Male Call

by

MILTON CANIFF

1942-1946

FEATURING
MISS LACE

EDITED BY
PETER POPLASKI

KITCHEN SINK PRESS

Princeton   Wisconsin

ISBN 0-87816-026-4 (hardcover)
ISBN 0-87816-027-2 (softcover)

The publisher wishes to express his gratitude to the following people for preparing *Milton Caniff's Male Call* for publication. **Lucy Caswell**, of the Ohio State University Milton Caniff Research Center, provided proofs of all the strips printed. **Jan Manweiler** helped with production. **Dave Schreiner** transcribed, edited and typeset "The Two Minute Furlough." **Peter Poplaski** edited the book and coordinated its production. **Bill Mauldin** graciously consented to write the Foreword. **Finally, Milton Caniff** created this work and cooperated fully in this edition.

Fourth printing January 1989

If you like *Male Call*, you may want to subscribe to *Milton Caniff's Steve Canyon Magazine*, which reprints in chronology the entire adventure which began in 1947. Subscriptions are $36 for six issues. Visa and Mastercard accepted. We also have available a free catalog of everything we publish, including books, magazines and fine comics. Address orders to Kitchen Sink Press, No. 2 Swamp Rd., Princeton WI 54968.

"Joe, yestiddy ya saved my life an' I swore I'd pay ya back. Here's my last pair of dry socks."

FOREWORD

by Bill Mauldin

Today's young TV addicts have no idea what comic strips meant to kids in my day (late Twenties and early Thirties). This was especially true in rural areas. My family didn't even own a radio. Comics were all we had in the way of pictorial entertainment: our sole escape from the humdrum of farm life. My older brother and I used to race each other home from school, leaping ditches and ripping our pants on barbed-wire fences, to beat each other to the comics page of the day's newspaper. Any trick to delay the other guy was allowable, and some of our best (or worst) fist fights resulted from this.

The creators of those comic strips ranked, in celebrity and pay, with the top movie stars of the era. We're talking thousands of dollars a week at a time when Henry Ford shocked the industrial world by paying auto workers the princely sum of five dollars a day, eggs were a dime a dozen, and shoes were two dollars a pair. Is it any wonder that hard-scrabble country boys such as myself aspired to be cartoonists? (I thought of becoming a movie star but the mirror talked me out of that notion).

My own favorites among the giants of the comic strip world were Milton Caniff (*Terry and the Pirates*), Al Capp (*Li'l Abner*), Roy Crane (*Wash Tubbs*), and Hal Foster, who did an exquisitely-drawn version of *Tarzan of the Apes*. There were other good strips but I considered these the cream of the crop—an opinion shared by most readers, evidently. (I believe Chic Young's *Blondie* was the circulation leader, bringing its creator an incredible half-million dollars or so annually, but these other guys weren't far behind).

Caniff was my particular favorite because I learned much about drawing from studying his strip. Later, after World War II, when we became friends (and neighbors by chance), I was able to pay Milton back in a small way by teaching him how to slant the windshield on a jeep and slope the back side of the heel on a cowboy boot. But minor slants and slopes were nothing compared to what I had gotten from him in my formative years: composition, lights and shadow, dramatic angles—everything down to the wrinkles in a coat sleeve. Thanks to studying Milton's work, I eventually even learned to draw passably pretty women: something I had always craved to do.

Which brings us to Miss Lace, probably the most delectable pen-and-ink creation of all time, the camp follower of every fighting man's dreams. Caniff, an aviation buff and devout patriot, was kept by physical disability from being either pilot or soldier, so he did it all at his drawing board. And what a job he did! A master of research and keeper of voluminous reference files, with *Terry and the Pirates* he conducted a paper war so deadly accurate and perspicacious, strategy-wise, that military intelligence went nuts trying to figure out how he always stayed a jump ahead of the Pentagon and finally made him an official "war industry" so they could post agents on his property. Presumably this kept enemy agents from peeking over his shoulder.

At a time when Hollywood publicists were creating fortunes from "pinups" such as Rita Hayworth and Betty Grable, Caniff produced in Miss Lace a confection of femininity which put them all into the shade, and he never realized a nickel's profit from her. He created and drew Lace in weekly installments for free distribution to the military press: *Stars and Stripes* and *Yank* for the army and similar publications for other branches. The comic strip (what a pitifully inadequate name for it!) went by the name of *Male Call*. Officially his audience numbered some 15 million servicemen, but military newspapers and magazines were read by countless civilians, too, so there is no way of estimating the actual audience. By the end of the war, *Male Call* appeared regularly in some 3,000 publications.

Mind you, Caniff created Miss Lace weekly on top of drawing six regular daily *Terry* strips, plus a full-color Sunday page. Almost alone among comics artists, Milton did nearly all of his own drawing. He had some help in filling backgrounds and lettering, but otherwise what came out of his ink bottle was half sweat. I can testify from my own observations as his post-war neighbor and midnight coffee consultant that he worked a 27-hour day and a 10-day week. To pile another strip on top of all this must have been a staggering task, but as Milton liked to put it, those who say creative work is harder than digging ditches have never dug ditches. Or foxholes.

Just as it's impossible to figure Miss Lace's World War II audience, there's no way to measure the cumulative intensity of feeling she generated. If you've never met her before, study this perky little vision of pulchritudity who is now celebrating what must be approximately her 65th birthday. She is as fresh, stylish, titillating, saucy, sexy and delightful as ever, and if today you happen to be a lonely young man assigned to duty in some dank jungle or dusty desert and if you didn't know Lace's age, wouldn't she turn you on? Hell, she'd turn you on if you *did* know her age.

June 1, 1987
New Mexico

"Just gimme a coupla aspirin. I already got a Purple Heart."

BILL MAULDIN WON HIS FIRST OF TWO PULITZER PRIZES AS A 23-YEAR-OLD EDITORIAL CARTOONIST FOR 'STARS AND STRIPES,' THE OVERSEAS MILITARY NEWSPAPER. SGT. MAULDIN'S ART MOST OFTEN CENTERED ON TWO "DOGFACE" FRONT LINE ENLISTED MEN, WILLIE AND JOE, WHO SPOKE FOR ALL THE FIGHTING MEN. (1944).

6. YOU CAN HELP

'WHAT TO DO IN AN AIR RAID.' FINAL PANEL. (1941)

THE TWO-MINUTE FURLOUGH

with Milton Caniff

In the late 1930s and in 1940, while I was doing *Terry and the Pirates*, I had begun to anticipate the fact that the United States was headed for war. You didn't have to be a scholar of events to see it coming, even though everyone wanted it *not* to come. The Japanese weren't helping matters. They really didn't know what they were getting into, either. Little did they realize that they were about to waken the sleeping giant, as the phrase had it. *Terry and the Pirates* was set in China, and the Japanese had been at war there for years. In the strip I viewed them as an obtrusive invader of the China that existed then. I didn't call them Japanese, just "the invaders," but I made no attempt to conceal the fact that the invaders were straight, out-and-out Japanese troops. Joseph Patterson, the publisher of the *New York Daily News* and the boss of my syndicate, didn't want politics to show up on the comics page, so the strip wasn't as involved in what was happening as I would have liked. I went as far with it as I could, but the general reader didn't think in terms of politics. This was just an adventure, and the real life overtones did not become evident until December 7, 1941, when the Japanese bombed Pearl Harbor.

Before that happened, everyone was anticipating a war involving us breaking out in a big hurry *somewhere*. Europe had been fighting Hitler since 1939, after all. The National Defense people asked me to do a poster on what would happen if we were bombed. It was distributed on the west coast the day after Pearl Harbor, so that's how close everybody was to feeling the war was coming our way.

The poster was one of the very earliest of my special drawings for military and defense use. At that point, any means were used to inform, recruit and raise morale. It got more concentrated later on, when the hotshots in the newspaper and advertising business began to migrate to Washington, but at the beginning, there was very little. But well before Pearl Harbor, I had been thinking that there must be something I could do for the troops. Having been in boys' camps, I knew the need for anything to read for morale purposes or whatever.

I also knew that I was going to be 4F; I'd already been through that with my doctor. Back in the 1920s, I had contracted phlebitis from an insect bite, which causes an inflammation in the blood vessels in the legs and can lead to blood clots. I still have it to this day. I was drafted twice. Out in the country where I was living, they reached the bottom of their draft pool early. I got called and went in for my physical, got examined and certified, and was thrown out. Late in the war, they reached the bottom of the pool again, and I was

called in, and this time the doctor just automatically put me on the 4F status. But I knew from the beginning that I'd be sitting out the war, and I felt guilty as hell about it. Bill Mauldin, who I got to know later after he came back from the European theater, called it "homefront neurosis." The result was, I wanted badly to do some work for the guys who had to fight; something *just* for them.

When the war started, both Al Capp and I volunteered to do whatever we could. Our first assignment was to do cautionary posters about venereal disease. They turned down my poster because the bad girls were too good looking. They turned down Al's because he overplayed it a bit. They knew he had the audience out there and they were anxious to get him involved, but he couldn't quite find the handle they wanted. The trouble was, they wanted to be specific about condoms, but not *too* specific. They could get drawings done by somebody who wasn't well known, and that could illustrate the little book the chaplain or medic gave you. If they had a well-known cartoonist like Al, the poster he did would almost defeat itself. The men would be looking at Li'l Abner and what he said about it, ha ha ha, instead of the message. That was true of mine, too. I didn't use the *Terry* characters, but the people in it were obviously right out of the strip, including the bad girls.

Al and I both blew it, but that was the beginning. I had begun to think of doing something on a regular basis for the camp newspapers that were springing up everywhere. Right then, they were mostly mimeographed sheets, and I knew that their editors were hard put to fill them each week. If I could supply a strip every week, I could help them out. A friend of mine in Washington reacted very warmly to the idea, so we began to work out the procedure for getting the strip off the ground and distributed.

They were going to channel the distribution through *Yank* magazine, which had its offices on 42nd Street in New York. However, they couldn't just accept work by civilians in *Yank*, so they established what they called the Camp Newspaper Service, which is on all the proofsheets. That was the area where they could accept civilian work. There was no money involved, of course. It wasn't a matter of who pays what; it was just a matter of acceptance on the part of the editors. There were enough professionals involved that saw the point of what I was doing. They saw the need.

The officer in charge was Col. Franklin Forsberg. Everybody else on the staff was enlisted. They included Herblock, who had already won a Pulitzer Prize, and Sgt. George Baker, who created *Sad Sack*. It was a talented bunch. The editor was Joseph McCarthy, not the senator, who was from Boston. They arranged with the A.B. Dick Co. to put out, for every camp newspaper, a mimeograph stencil of just my accepted line drawing. Then they would send the drawing back to me, and I'd add the blacks and send it back for them to make mats for the camp papers that had more sophisticated equipment. So I did two versions. Eventually, the strip went to 3,000 newspapers — oh, what a syndication!

On occasion, one of my strips would be rejected by Forsberg. He never gave much of a reason; just a pencil note of "No" on the strip itself. I suppose some of them were a bit racy, and some of them reflected poorly on the military, they thought. I never questioned or challenged them, because I simply didn't have the time. I wasn't getting paid for it, so I could have, but I just sent them another.

To have all this happen, I had to be a number of weeks ahead. I started the strip in the summer of 1942 and the first release was in October. A real problem was delivering them. It's hard to imagine today what a tough thing it was to get that damn strip into New York from my place in the country. Gas rationing was in effect, but fortunately I had to deliver six daily strips and a Sunday *Terry* page across the street at the Daily News building at the same time. I sent a high school boy on the train after school and he came right back on the next train. He usually just made it by 5 p.m., right before both places closed. He'd come to my house on his bike, pick up the originals, and catch the train for New York. Sometimes he'd miss the train coming back, and his parents would be upset, of course, but he never missed a delivery. Big, awful stuff, travel in that day.

It turned out that it was good I had so much lead time, because we had trouble with the strip at the beginning. I began

DRAGON LADY CHRISTMAS
CARD (left) AND PIN-UP (1939)

by calling it *Terry and the Pirates* and featured Burma as the lead. An early effort was taken from a 1939 Christmas card I had done, which showed Terry and Pat being served food by half-nude serving girls, and with the Dragon Lady delivering the line about the "food being too spicy for you." The key to the story was the switching of the Dragon Lady with Burma.

Burma was an American, and I thought she would appeal more to the Americans. The Dragon Lady was great, but unapproachable. With Burma, it was always "maybe." Sadie Thompson, from Somerset Maugham's play *Rain*, was the inspiration for her. She and Burma were good time girls. When I had done some pinups before this time of both Burma and the Dragon Lady, the Burma pinups all went and I was left with a stack of Dragon Ladies. The only explanation I can think of is that having the Dragon Lady pinup was kind of a private thing to put in your own room or something. On the other hand, the Rita Hayworth type of pinup everybody could enjoy, and the Burma art was like that. You could put her up in the rec room or whatever. Everybody's girl friend; everybody's wet dream. That's why I used her.

The military did not say anything about what the strip should be titled. They accepted it because the individual editors of the camp papers were ecstatic to start with that much copy. But the Army Air Force had a big training area near Miami Beach, and their paper was printed at a local job shop. It happened that the same shop printed the Miami Beach civilian paper, and they started using my camp version of *Terry and the Pirates*. That's when it hit the fan.

The publisher of the *Miami Herald*, John Knight, who was printing the regular version of the strip, complained to the syndicate. I got a call from the manager of the syndicate, who really chewed me out, and told me to stop immediately. So I had to tell the camp papers I had to stop.

The flap it caused seems almost amusing today. It wasn't then. I was called in by the publisher, Patterson, and here I was back again with the old man. No mention at all of "the invaders." That was all in the past. He didn't call me in for a personal interview. The syndicate manager, the guy who had given me hell, called me in and said the boss had a message for me. He said I was to continue this thing for the war effort, but change the name, which is the big objection, and change the woman. That's all, just go ahead. Patterson had been an artilleryman in World War I, and he knew exactly what I was trying to do. The manager of the syndicate didn't know beans about the trenches in France or someplace, but the boss

PORTRAIT OF BURMA (1937)

11

**BURMA
(1936)**

did.

He gave me the green light, and when I informed the camp papers, they were delighted.

When I started up again, the camp newspapers named the strip *Male Call*. The Miss Lace part was my contribution; I wanted a short, sexy name. The newspapers wanted an overall title, and they came up with *Male Call*. I was glad for the suggestion, because it fit perfectly. When I fashioned Miss Lace, I wanted someone who was the opposite of Burma, so right away, I gave her black hair. I viewed her as innocent but sexy as hell—much more so than the standard of the day. I was on pioneering ground here, because I wanted her to have "it" without being overt.

In the end, she was not like Burma at all. A big factor was that we were dealing with a girl you knew nothing about. In the background, you already had a pretty good picture of Burma, that she was anybody's girl friend. Lace was never anybody's girl friend, really. She might be playing poker with you, but she won't necessarily be going to bed with you.

But if you played your cards right, just *maybe, maybe, maybe*. The "maybe" is always better than the accomplishment; there's that anticipation of what's ahead. I began to realize after I got into it that the unattainable nature of Lace was more useful over the long haul than portraying somebody that you knew had been in the hay with the lieutenant over the weekend. That's a big difference.

I didn't base Lace on any movie stars. She was the visualization of an idea, a point of view. It was as if she was a genie, a waif, who appeared in your dreams. When she turned the tables on some hot pants GI, or the hot pants colonel for that matter, it was fun. It was a wish fulfillment for the readers. She was always there, always available, and yet *not* available. The whole thing hung on the point of view of the American GI, the American guy suddenly dumped in a place he'd never heard of before. What he's really thinking about is the girl back home, not the tavern wench near the air base in England. That's for officers, anyway. So all he can think about is miss so and so back home. There are a number of kissing scenes in the strips, which was the kind of thing that most guys would have loved to have happened. But they never expected it to happen in reality, and so that's where the dreams came in. It was a wish fulfillment, and in a way, it was in the nature of a two minute furlough back home for the guys when they read the strip.

Reaction to *Male Call* was very good. And I got a *lot* of fan mail about Miss Lace. The first reaction I got was from

**MISS LACE
(1943)**

SEX HYGIENE

SAD SACK
(1943)

SGT. GEORGE BAKER

Li'l Abner . . . By Al Capp.

SPECIAL "LI'L ABNER" POSTER FOR THE ARMY MORALE SERVICES DIVISION BY AL CAPP. 12/13/43

the editors of the camp newspapers. They were so relieved to have it back in the papers. They said it sparkled up their papers, but more than that, it gave them something unique. "The local newspaper doesn't have this. They *can't* have it." It gave them a sense of pride. I did not think of that in the beginning; they reminded me of it themselves. "We'll show the *Chicago Tribune*. We've got something the boys *really* want to read."

I did not get much mail from the GIs suggesting gags. Surprisingly enough, I think they felt that I was ahead of them, and they just wanted to sit back and be entertained. Most of my letters were the appreciative type. "Thank you very much. Keep 'em coming." It's usually the other way around, with letters pointing out that something that occurred in a strip happened to the writer last month. That didn't happen, probably because *Male Call* was so offbeat. There was nobody around like Lace to say those lines, there wasn't that parallel in their lives.

There was some negative mail, but so little that it really didn't matter. When you have a syndication of 3,000 papers, nobody argues. Besides that, most of the civilians who saw it realized it was for the guys. The civilians who did complain about its raciness were told by the War Department that "this is for the guys, and not for you, Lady Jane. It is done for the boys and that is where it shall stay." I never got into trouble because something was dirty. It was suggestive, but not dirty. I regard it as a clean strip.

The few complaints I got from the readers had to do with accuracy in uniforms and such. I once depicted some sailors in dress white uniforms with blue collars, which, since my home wasn't near any sort of Naval base, I got from a book. I got an official Navy letter from an admiral that said, "Since the outbreak of present hostilities, naval personnel do not wear the dress white uniform with blue collar. Watch that stuff, bud." In *Terry*, I depicted the cross on a chaplain's uniform canted in the wrong direction. I should have known better, because the canting of the cross was supposed to suggest that the chaplain was bearing it. I heard from many chaplains about that, and they can give you more hell than anybody.

But most of the time, when I needed research material, the military would send it over. There was a big debarkation center called Camp Shanks fairly near my home, and if I needed something right this minute, they could pull somebody out and send him over in a jeep. They had the fuel. The air force stuff came from West Point, which at that time was trying to teach cadets to fly. I did my research at night, and it was

a very busy time. Sometimes I didn't even take my pajamas off for a couple days, and my wife, Bunny, sometimes wondered if I'd ever get upstairs.

Male Call wasn't done on a schedule. That was the hell of it. It was done during lunch hours and at odd times, and it eventually became harder to do than *Terry and the Pirates*. Frank Engli, my letterer, and Raymond Bailey, who worked on backgrounds and did research for me, helped on all the things I was working on at this time. But it was hard all the same.

My schedule for *Terry* called for writing it on Monday, pencilling it on Tuesday, inking on Wednesday and the backgrounds on Thursday. I could always pull the camera away from Terry himself, and I had a continuity going in which one strip could help write the next.

Not so with *Male Call*. Each one had to be a self-contained gag; a continuity wouldn't work because with guys moving around all the time, it wouldn't be possible for them to keep up. They all had to have a military angle, so I'd spend my lunchtime fishing for that. I had to pick out a branch of the service or an activity, or an item like a jeep and do a whole strip around that. I have a strip where some guys are riding a jeep and they see Miss Lace and the *jeep* starts chasing her. All that began with my saying, "I want to do something about a jeep." But getting the gag together around a military angle was sometimes an agony.

I started with the last panel first, the punchline. I've always *drawn* the last panel first and worked my way backwards simply because I am lefthanded and I didn't want to smear my hand over something that was already drawn. But the tough part is in the first three panels. The enormously important part is, "how do I get off this page?" The build up has to be smooth without giving anything away, but *everything* has to be in those four panels.

I also did *Male Call* strips about wounded GIs, including amputees and blind men. About every four months during the war, I would tour veterans' hospitals with other cartoonists, guys like Rube Goldberg, who was too old to serve, and guys like me who were 4F and had this feeling of guilt about it. The homefront neurosis again. We called it the Purple Heart circuit. These tours didn't give me any specific ideas for strips, but they were the inspiration for some. I remember well giving a chalk talk for some blind veterans at an Atlantic City hospital. The administrators asked me to do it, and it scared the hell out of me. The people who asked me said that "before all these guys became blind, they were fans of your stuff. You

say, 'I'm drawing a picture of the Dragon Lady,' and they know what you're talking about. Don't be afraid of our guys." And it was true; exactly that. They reacted and even applauded at times. I'd say, "I'm putting the upper lip on her now, then the lower lip," and they were right with it. If you hadn't known they were blind, you wouldn't have known they were blind. It was the toughest crowd I ever faced; not for them, but for *me*.

We were so busy with all this stuff that it's hard to imagine now how occupied we were. But in 1945 and 1946, things started winding down. Just as you could see the war coming, you could also see it ending at last. You could feel it. The Camp Newspaper Service began losing subscribers; the boys were drifting back home, slowly at first, and then in a rush. Eventually, *Male Call* took on a civilian overtone, and soon after, I retired it.

After the war, I kept getting requests for portraits of Miss Lace from groups having reunions. I did a number of them for the Air Force Association for their booklets, and I always put her in a current context. She would be talking about the meeting in St. Louis, or wherever, and they would feature her on the cover of the booklet. Some of those drawings got pretty raunchy for the time. It was considered pretty snappy stuff.

But for the most part, Miss Lace and *Male Call* went back into the inkwell after the World War. The strip is frozen in time. It served its purpose, and I did not revive it for the Korean or Vietnam Wars. *Male Call* is available always, but on a World War level only.

May 24, 1987
New York, New York

SPECIAL DRAWING FOR A BLOOD DONOR PROGRAM (1945). LEFT: CANIFF SELF-PORTRAIT (1942).

Terry And The Pirates

MISSY BURMA, LONG TIME NO SEE MIST' TERRY LEE AN' MIST' PAT RYAN!

THEY'RE PROBABLY OUT DIVIDING BY ZEROS! BUT THERE ARE PLENTY OF AMERICAN GENTS IN CHINA NOW... I WONDER IF THOSE BRASS BUTTONS GET AS COLD AS THEY USED TO BE? SEE WHO'S AT THE DOOR!

HIM ASK TO SEE LADY OF HOUSE!

WHAT'S BROILIN' SOLDIER?

IT'S THIS WAY, MA'M... THE MEN OF MY UNIT THINK OF ME AS THE STUDIOUS TYPE...

I NEVER TOUCH THE STUFF MYSELF— BUT DO GO ON...

IT IS MY THEORY THAT INTENSE STUDY OF TERRAIN IS OF GREAT VALUE TO THE MILITARY MAN... SINCE ARRIVING IN THIS AREA, I HAVE CONCENTRATED ON THE LOCAL GEOGRAPHY...

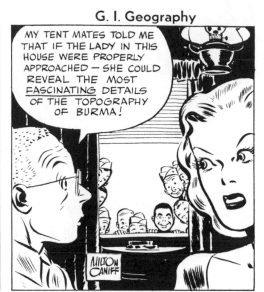

MY TENT MATES TOLD ME THAT IF THE LADY IN THIS HOUSE WERE PROPERLY APPROACHED — SHE COULD REVEAL THE MOST FASCINATING DETAILS OF THE TOPOGRAPHY OF BURMA!

Reg. U. S. Pat. Off.:
Copyright, 1942, by News Syndicate Co. Inc.

MILTON CANIFF

10/11/42

Terry And The Pirates

MISSY BURMA CALL?

YEAH... THOSE SOLDIERS MAY BE HAVIN' TROUBLE WITH THE CHINESE FOOD WHEN THEY'RE OUT ON THE TOWN! I'M GONNA ASK A COUPLE UP FOR A FEED!

THE CAPTAIN SAID YOU INVITED ANY TWO GUYS UP FOR DINNER, MA'AM! WE'RE IT!

OKAY, BOYS, COME IN AND TIE ON THE FEED BAG!

MILTON CANIFF

WHY DON'T YOU GUYS EAT? IS SOMETHING TOO SPICY?

Reg. U. S. Pat. Off.:
Copyright, 1942, by News Syndicate Co. Inc.

10/18/42

Terry And The Pirates

Terry And The Pirates

Terry And The Pirates

Neat Article Of War

11/8/42

Terry And The Pirates

Slow Fire; Prone From Standing

11/15/42

Terry And The Pirates

Wench In The Machinery Of War

11-22-42

11/22/42

Terry And The Pirates

Sweet Pickin's

11/29/42

11/29/42

Terry And The Pirates

Praise The Lord—Look Who's In The Kitchen

12/6/42

Terry and The Pirates

Check Points For Contact Flying

12/13/42

Terry And The Pirates

Two Low Pairs, Natural

12/20/42

Terry and The Pirates

Patrol Fails To Contact Main Body

12/27/42

Terry and The Pirates

Booby Trap

Terry and The Pirates

Snif Test Indicates Odor Of Chanel No. 5

24

"SOLID SENDER" WAS THE LAST "BURMA" STRIP CANIFF DREW WITH THE "TERRY" TITLE. IT HAD ALREADY BEEN APPROVED BY THE MILITARY AND SENT TO THE A.B. DICK CO. TO BE MADE INTO A STENCIL FOR MIMEOGRAPH REPRODUCTION WHEN THE SYNDICATE CALLED A HALT TO THE STRIP. IT WAS NEVER RELEASED IN THIS VERSION. WHEN HE WAS LATER ALLOWED TO CONTINUE THE FEATURE UNDER A DIFFERENT TITLE AND CHARACTER LEAD, CANIFF REINKED THE FIGURE AS MISS LACE.

MADAME
SHOO - SHOO

ALWAYS ON THE RUN FROM BRITISH AUTHORITIES, BURMA OFTEN USED AN ALIAS IN "TERRY AND THE PIRATES." FORCED FROM HER OWN SPECIAL STRIP, SHE ONCE AGAIN TURNED UP IN "TERRY" AS MADAME SHOO SHOO, AN EXOTIC DANCER NOT ONLY ENTERTAINING THE TROOPS THIS TIME, BUT THE GENERAL PUBLIC AS WELL.

MEANWHILE...IN LATE 1942, CANIFF STARTED PRODUCING "MALE CALL" AND A CERTAIN MISS LACE BEGAN SCORING WITH ALL THE MEN AT WAR.

Male Call

by Milton Caniff, creator of "Terry and the Pirates"

Pillow Fight

1/24/43

Male Call

by Milton Caniff, creator of "Terry and the Pirates"

Long Overdue—Must Be Considered Lost

1/31/43

Male Call

by Milton Caniff, creator of "Terry and the Pirates"

Moral: Keep Your Brass Warm

DEPLOY AS SKOIMISHERS! HERE COMES McGOOLTY!

DON'T MURDER HIM TILL WE FIND OUT THE NAME OF THAT NEW DOLL WHO MOVED IN DOWN THE ROAD...

SHE SAID HER FRIENDS JUST CALL HER "LACE"... SHE WOULDN'T TELL ME ANY MORE... SO I LEFT!

OKAY, McGOOLTY! WE'LL LET YOU LIVE!

DAT McGOOLTY!... HE'S GONE ALL DIS TIME — AND ALL HE FINDS OUT IS DAT DIS NEW CHICK'S NAME IS "LACE"! AIN'T HE GOT NO EN-TUH-PRICE?

WELL...

For General McGoolty

Oh, Mac — those cold buttons! thine — Lace

COPYRIGHT 1943 by MILTON CANIFF

2/7/43

Male Call

by Milton Caniff, creator of "Terry and the Pirates"

Solid Sender

WHAT'S THE MATTER WITH THAT G. I. JOKER OVER THERE?

A BATCH OF MAIL CAME IN TODAY — HE'S THE ONLY GUY IN THE OUTFIT WHO GOT NO LETTER!

NO LETTER, HUH SOJER?

AW — THE FOLKS ARE PRETTY BUSY WITH ALL KINDS OF STUFF THESE DAYS... THEY'D WRITE IF THEY HAD TIME...

MILTON CANIFF

TELL THOSE A.P.O. JOES YOU PLAYED A LITTLE PRIVATE POST OFFICE... AND THERE ARE THE STAMPS TO PROVE IT! DELIVER YOURSELF TO MY ADDRESS TONIGHT! ...THERE WON'T BE ANY OTHER MALE AROUND TO KEEP YOU FROM REGISTERING!

COPYRIGHT 1943 by MILTON CANIFF

2/14/43

Male Call

Zest in OTS

CAPTAIN, I'M WORRIED ABOUT THE FAILURE OF THE MEN TO IDENTIFY AIRCRAFT SILHOUETTES

WE HAVE A NEW LECTURE SYSTEM, ON THAT, SIR...

THE MEN COMBINED THEIR PIN-UP PICTURES WITH RECOGNITION CHARTS—THERE'S A DEMONSTRATION ON RIGHT NOW...

SING IT OUT, YOU JOKERS!

BULL-NECK BESSIE! SOVIET I-16B

ROUND-NOSE ROSIE! MITSUBISHI 00

FAT-WAIST FANNY! C-46 COMMANDO

BOX-KITE BETTY P-38 LIGHTNING

FULL-FLAP FLORENCE! AICHI 99

WHAT DO YOU THINK, SIR?

VERY INTERESTING! I—AH—BELIEVE I'LL STAY AND BRUSH UP ON THOSE SHA--- I MEAN OUTLINES, MYSELF...

Copyright 1943 by

MILTON CANIFF

2/21/43

Male Call

Peepsight

...THE COLONEL'S COMPLIMENTS MA'AM—AND WOULD YOU CARE TO CROSS OVER AND WATCH THE PARADE FROM THE REVIEWING STAND?

DON'T MIND IF I DO... I WAS ABOUT TO TAKE OFF DOWNWIND...

THE OLD MAN'S NO SLOW JOE...HE INVITED THE LACE GAL ACROSS THE STREET TO THE PLATFORM...

HE'S JUST LOOKING TO THE WELFARE OF HIS MEN...

THE FIRST BATTALION THAT PASSED IN REVIEW IS NOW OVER BEING TREATED FOR CROSSED EYES!

MILTON CANIFF

COPYRIGHT 1943 by

2/28/43

29

Male Call

by Milton Caniff, Creator of "Terry and the Pirates"

Wipe That Opinion Off Your Face

3/7/43

Male Call

by Milton Caniff Creator of 'Terry and the Pirates"

Flank Exposed: Troops Vulnerable

3/14/43

Male Call

by Milton Caniff, Creator of "Terry and the Pirates"

Lackey in Khaki Goes WAACY

3/21/43

Male Call

by Milton Caniff, Creator of "Terry and the Pirates"

Blanket Roll

3/28/43

Male Call

by Milton Caniff, Creator of "Terry and the Pirates"

Something Hot at the PX

4/4/43

Male Call

by Milton Caniff Creator of "Terry and the Pirates" ## ... But The Situation Is Well In Hand

4/11/43

Male Call

by Milton Caniff, Creator of "Terry and the Pirates"

Wearing Pinks, No Doubt

4/18/43

Male Call

by Milton Caniff, Creator of "Terry and the Pirates"

Television Snafu

4/25/43

Male Call

Wrong Jive—Take Five

EXCELLENCE! IS YANKEE CODE MESSAGE!

SO?

Hiya, Johnny One Stripe!
Just to let you know the steam is still beamed your way—Action, Jaxon!
I'm staying out from under the apple bush—and I don't want to hear that you reached like a leech for some peach on a beach.
Kipper the Nipper till its MUR-der, he says—Meanwhile, no nation of passion in these parts—but when the 4-F's come around I say, "Stay away from my block, Buster!". You have to be under arms before you get into mine"
Finish that thing and get back. There's something about you that makes my joints jump.
Your 5 feet 5—Alive as a hive
Dottie

...I LEARN YANKEE TALK FROM CROSSED WORD PUZZLE! CODE MESSAGE PLAINLY SAYS: VESSEL NAMED "JAXON" STEAMS TOWARD YANKEE BEACH-HEAD... "KIPPER" IS YANKEE SUBMARINE, WHICH ARE NAMED FOR FISH... BLOCK BUSTER BOMBS WILL BE USED TIME OF ATTACK IS 5:05!

AH! THEN WE ATTACK AT 4:30!

04:36

YOU AND YOUR 源裕永 CROSSED WORD PUZZLES!

COPYRIGHT 1943 by—

5/2/43

Male Call

Reviewing Party: Arms Stacked

LET UP, WILLYA SARGE? ME BACK IS BROKE!

F'PETE'S SAKE, SARGE!

OKAY— WE'LL FINISH T'MORROW!

U.S. ARMY

COPYRIGHT 1943 by MILTON CANIFF

LATER

WELL—IF IT AIN'T MISS LACE!

GREETIN'S AN' SALLOWTASHUNS, MISS LACE!

OH, I'M GLAD TO SEE YOU GENERALS...

I JUST BOUGHT SOME THINGS I NEED IN A HURRY... WILL YOU CARRY THEM HOME FOR ME?

WE'RE D' BEST IN D' BUSINESS

FOIST CLASS!

WHAT'S THE MATTER, BOYS? SOMETHING YOU ATE?

TOMORROW IS ANOTHER DAY...

MILTON CANIFF

5/9/43

Male Call

by Milton Caniff, Creator of "Terry and the Pirates"

This Took Crust

5/16/43

Male Call
Milton Caniff, Creator of "Terry and the Pirates" **Moral: Have Right Eye Open When You Squeeze**

5/23/43

Male Call

by Milton Caniff, Creator of "Terry and the Pirates"

What The Newsreel Did Not Show

COPYRIGHT 1943 by

5/30/43

Male Call

by Milton Caniff, Creator of "Terry and the Pirates"

Fever Communicated By Contact

6/6/43

Male Call

by Milton Caniff, Creator of "Terry and the Pirates"

Quite A Battle Sight

6/13/43

Male Call

by Milton Caniff, Creator of "Terry and the Pirates"

The Boy In Upper 13

6/20/43

Male Call

by Milton Caniff, Creator of "Terry and the Pirates"

Auxiliary Power

6/27/43

Male Call

by Milton Caniff, Creator of "Terry and the Pirates"

Flank Coverage

7/4/43

Male Call

by Milton Caniff, Creator of "Terry and the Pirates"

Ranks For The Memory

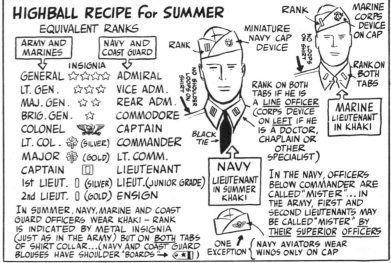

Male Call

by Milton Caniff, Creator of 'Terry and the Pirates''

BIMEBY SLAP-SLAP

7/11/43

7/18/43

Male Call

by Milton Caniff, Creator of "Terry and the Pirates"

Edging The Dredging With Lace

7/25/43

Male Call

by Milton Caniff, Creator of "Terry and the Pirates"

Whoops Group

8/1/43

40

Male Call

by Milton Caniff, Creator of "Terry and the Pirates"

Stand By To Repel Side Boys

8/8/43

Male Call

by Milton Caniff, creator of Terry and the Pirates

Why Don't You Do Wright?

8/15/43

Male Call

by Milton Caniff, creator of Terry and the Pirates

Fire Control Manual

8/22/43

Male Call

by Milton Caniff, creator of Terry and the Pirates

Slight Snaf In Cupid's Path

8/29/43

Male Call

by Milton Caniff, creator of Terry and the Pirates

Go West, Young Man

Copyright 1943 by Milton Caniff, distributed by Camp Newspaper Service

9/5/43

Male Call

by Milton Caniff, creator of "Terry and the Pirates"

Drawn and Quotaed

Copyright 1943 by Milton Caniff, distributed by Camp Newspaper Service

9/12/43

Male Call

Magnetic Azimuth

WHAT'S EATING YOU, SERGEANT?

I HAD A DATE WITH MISS LACE, SIR...THEM GOONIES HEARD WE WUZ ALERTED AN' I HAD TO CANCEL...NOW THEY'RE GONNA GO AN' GRAB THE OPEN TIME!

SO LONG, SUCKUH!

GEEZST

KEEP YOUR SHIRT ON, SERGEANT!

I GIVE UP!.. IN A FOG LIKE THIS, EVEN CHRIS COLUMBUS COULDN'T FIND MISS LACE'S HOUSE!

Copyright 1943 by Milton Caniff, distributed by Camp Newspaper Service

9/19/43

Male Call

Dim View

YOU TANK JOCKEYS IS ALWAYS YAPPIN' ABOUT HOW RUGGED YOUR OUTFITS ARE! I SAY PHUD!

THE LIDDLE MAN THINKS WE'RE PHUDS! SHALL WE GIVE HIM A DRY RUN, MONTMORENCY?

YUH, THROCKBUTT, NOT A M.P. IN SIGHT!

1.

ME AN' MY CHUM MONTMORENCY AIMS TO SHOW YOU WHAT RIDIN' OUR RUMBLE BUGGIES IS LIKE...

2.

THEN Y' GET AN ORDER T' ADVANCE...

4.

FOIST WE'LL H'IST Y' INTA THIS DRUM —WHICH IS ABOUT HOW MUCH SPACE Y' HAVE IN A TANK

AN' ABOUT AS OILY!

3.

AN' TH' MACHINE GUNS OPEN ON YER ARMOR..

AN' TH' DUST BLOWS IN...

5.

6. AN' Y' DROP A FEW FEET CROSSIN' A DITCH....

AN' HIT TH' DRINK ALL UNBUTTONED...

D'YUH STILL THINK TANK JOCKEYS IS PHUDS, BUD?

GRACIOUS, THROCKBUTT, I DO BELIEVE OUR GUEST HAS COME DOWN WITH BOGIE FEVER!

7.

Copyright 1943 by Milton Caniff, distributed by Camp Newspaper Service

9/26/43

44

Male Call
by Milton Caniff, creator of "Terry and the Pirates"

It's All In The Way You Look At It

10/3/43

Male Call
by Milton Caniff, creator of "Terry and the Pirates"

There's A War On, Don't Be A 'No Show'

10/10/43

Male Call

by Milton Caniff, creator of "Terry and the Pirates"

It Was Rank

WOOSH! WHAT A NIGHT!

THASSA FACT, MISS LACE..OH, PHUD! THERE GOES MY LAST MATCH!

HEY! GOT A LIGHT BUD?

SURE...

WHAT'S THE MATTER? YOU DIDN'T LIKE THE PICTURE?

TOO MANY STARS!

10/17/43

Male Call

by Milton Caniff, creator of "Terry and the Pirates"

Like A Fetter From Home

MISS LACE TH' LITTLE GOONIE IS SO HOMESICK FOR HIS WIFE WE CAN'T DO NOTHIN' WITH HIM... HE WOULDN'T THINK OF ASKIN' YOU FOR A DATE—BUT I BROUGHT HIM 'CAUSE —YOU MIGHT KNOW HOW T' SNAP HIM OUT OF IT...

HMMM... THERE'S ONE THING THAT MIGHT WORK

10/24/43

THIS HERE'S MISS LACE!

H'LLLO!

WELL, I SEE YOU BOUGHT A CIGAR — BUT YOU DIDN'T THINK TO BRING ME ANYTHING!

HEY! DON'T SIT ON THE GOOD CHAIR!

WATCH THOSE ASHES!

MUST YOU ALWAYS LISTEN TO THE WAR NEWS? I WANNA DA-A-A-NCE!

—OH, YOU GOTTA GO ON DUTY!...I'VE HEARD THAT ONE BEFORE— G'NIGHT!

GEEZST, McGOOLTY, MISS LACE IS WUNNAFUL! —REMINDS ME SO MUCH OF MY GOITRUDE!

Male Call

by Milton Caniff creator of "Terry and the Pirates"

Elevation Not Corrected For Recoil

10/31/43

Male Call

by Milton Caniff, creator of "Terry and the Pirates"

Some Stuffing!

11/7/43

Male Call

Heart Chart

BASIC FIELD MANUAL (UNOFFICIAL)
JUNGLE WARFARE
(HOME FRONT VARIETY)

ACCLIMATION: IN JUNGLE WARFARE THE ENEMIES ARE MAN AND NATURE. WHEN YOU FIND YOURSELF ALONE, TAKE IT EASY — DON'T BECOME PANICKY...

DEFENSE: TRY THIS

OR THIS

SNAKES: THE DANGEROUS ONES ARE SOMETIMES HARD TO IDENTIFY AT FIRST (YOU CAN BE SURE WHEN THEY START TO COIL)

SIGNAL COMMUNICATION: SEMAPHORE AND WIGWAGGING MAY BRING FRIENDLY TROOPS

FRIENDLY NATIVES: BE CAREFUL — THEY MAY TURN YOU OVER TO THE ENEMY...

MENTAL ATTITUDE: IN THE ABSENCE OF YOUR C.O., USE YOUR IMAGINATION

LIQUIDS: BE SURE OF WHAT YOU DRINK — YOU MIGHT GET BOILED

VENOMOUS CREATURES OF MANY VARIETIES MAY BE ENCOUNTERED... DO THE RIGHT THING AND YOU HAVE NOTHING TO WORRY ABOUT...THIS BRAWL WON'T LAST FOREVER!

CLIP THIS AND SEND IT TO THAT CERTAIN PARTY. CIVILIANS DON'T HAVE ALL YOUR ADVANTAGES...

Copyright 1943 by Milton Caniff, distributed by Camp Newspaper Service

11/14/43

Male Call

Nick In The Tool Of War

WHEN AN OFFICUH ASKS YUH Y' NAME, YUH SAY, "PRIVATE SO-AN'-SO, SIR"...NOW WE'LL PRACTICE IT...WHAT'S Y' NAME, SOJER?

PRIVATE SO-AN'-SO, SAR-JINT!

NAW! Y'PRETEND I'M AN OFFICUH... AN' GIVE YUH OWN NAME!... NOW, WHAT'S YUH NAME, SOJER?

ORVILLE GUZZ...

LOOK!.. Y'STATE YUH GRADE FIRST! — THEN YUH SAY, "SIR", SEE? NOW, WHAT ARE YUH?

I'M HOMESICK, SIRSEE!

DON'T TAKE IT SO HARD, SARGE! — MEBBE THEY'LL LETCHA GO BACK T' NORTH AFRICA!

Copyright 1943 by Milton Caniff, distributed by Camp Newspaper Service

11/21/43

Male Call

by Milton Caniff, creator of "Terry and the Pirates"

You're Ridin', Now, Red!

with *deep bows to* Cpl. SANSONE — *the* ORIGINAL WOLF
Copyright 1943 by Milton Caniff, distributed by Camp Newspaper Service

11/28/43

Male Call

by Milton Caniff, creator of "Terry and the Pirates"

Bagged By A J.A.G.D.

Copyright 1943 by Milton Caniff, distributed by Camp Newspaper Service

12/5/43

Male Call

by Milton Caniff, creator of "Terry and the Pirates"

Tasty Dish On The T/O

WHAT'S THIS G-1, G-2, G-3, G-4 STUFF I'M ALWAYS HEARING ABOUT IN THE ARMY?

WELL, MISS LACE, EVERY COMMAND HAS FOUR FUNCTIONS—IT'S LIKE THIS...

...TO IMPOSE YOUR WILL ON PEOPLE, YOU GOTTA HAVE SOLDIERS LIKE ME, SEE! —THAT'S G-1, THE PERSONNEL SECTION—AND YOU ARE THE OBJECTIVE I WANTA ATTAIN!

G-2 IS MILITARY INTELLIGENCE—I GIVE YOU THE O.O., SEE THAT YOU'RE NOT CONVOYED, SIZE UP THE POSSIBILITIES, ESTIMATE MY CHANCES—AND MAP MY CAMPAIGN...

G-3 IS OPERATIONS AND TRAINING—I THROW MY TACTICAL FORCE INTO ACTION... I SAY, 'HIYA, BABE, WANTA SMOLDER ON A SOLDIER'S SHOULDER?'

...AND G-4 IS SUPPLY AND EVACUATION...

I GET IT! WHEN YOU FIND OUT HOW MUCH IT COSTS TO SUPPLY ME—THEN YOU EVACUATE!

12/12/43

Male Call

by Milton Caniff, creator of "Terry and the Pirates"

In Attacking, Never Take Terrain For Granted

SORRY, GENERALS, I CAN'T GO OUT WITH YOU TONIGHT... I HAVE A DATE WITH ONE OF THE BOYS IN THE 25th!

AW, GEEZST, MISS LACE...

THE 25th...THAT'S THE NEW OUTFIT WOT JUST MOVED IN! THEM GUYS GOT A NERVE COMMANDEERIN' OUR CHICK!

HEY—LET'S GET LOUIE'S CLIPPERS AN' NUDE-UP THAT GOONIE'S NOGGIN'! IT'LL LEARN THEM TWENTY-FIFTHS TO LAY OFF!

...HERE HE COMES!

LEAVE HIM HAVE IT!

12/19/43

Male Call

by Milton Caniff, creator of "Terry and the Pirates"

Combat Report

12/26/43

Male Call

by Milton Caniff, creator of "Terry and the Pirates"

Things Are Not Always As They Seam

1/2/44

Male Call

by Milton Caniff, creator of "Terry and the Pirates"

Briefs For Mission

HIYA MISS LACE?

TOL'ABLE, McGOOLTY ABLE TO PUTTER AND MUTTER...

WHAT WHIPS YOUR CORPUSCLES INTO SUCH A BRIGHT-EYED LOOK TODAY, GENERAL?

WELL...

I CAME TO SEE IF YOU WEAR PANTIES AND A BRASSIERE...

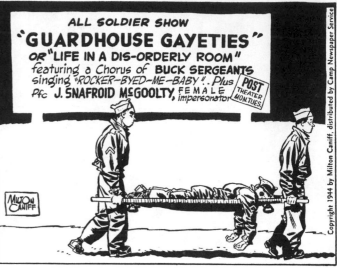

ALL SOLDIER SHOW "GUARDHOUSE GAYETIES" OR "LIFE IN A DIS-ORDERLY ROOM" featuring a Chorus of BUCK SERGEANTS singing "ROCKER-BYED-ME-BABY". Plus Pfc J. SNAFROID McGOOLTY, FEMALE impersonator

POST THEATER MON. TUES.

Copyright 1944 by Milton Caniff, distributed by Camp Newspaper Service

1/9/44

Male Call

by Milton Caniff, creator of "Terry and the Pirates"

Quarantine

SURE GLAD YOU'RE GOIN' OUT WITH US TONIGHT, MISS LACE! THEM DOGFACES CUT IN ON US WHEN WE'RE AT SEA...

FOOF! I LIKE ALL YOU FIGHTING GUYS....

COME SOLDIER WITH PACKAGE FOR MISSY...

....IT'S FROM THE SIGNAL CORPS GENERALS I HAD TO TURN DOWN FOR A DATE WHEN YOU BLUE JUMPER JOES TIED UP...

WHY— IT'S A GARTER...MADE OF LITTLE SIGNAL FLAGS! DOES IT SPELL OUT SOMETHING?

YEAH! IT SAYS, "OUT OF BOUNDS, ADMIRAL"

Copyright 1944 by Milton Caniff, distributed by Camp Newspaper Service

1/16/44

Male Call

by Milton Caniff, creator of "Terry and the Pirates"

Skimmer Primer

UNCLE SAM — hatter....

HIS VARIETY OF ISSUE HEADGEAR IS EXCEEDED ONLY BY THE WAYS G.I. JOE AND JOSEPHINE HAVE FOUND TO WEAR THEIR SHAP-PO

POOPED DROOP
one thing about this lid — it was good to sit on during 10 minute breaks...

CHINA-SIDE JOB-VERY MASKEE... only seagoin' Gyrenes with hash to the elbow can do this justice...

They never seemed to finish the NAVY NURSE'S hat...

THAT FIELD CAP ISN'T BUILT FOR THE R.A.F.'S PICCADILLY TILT — ESPECIALLY ON WINDY DAYS...

NAVY'S DISHPAN... who wouldn't wear earphones? It gets lonely in there — you can pick up Bob Hope between Zeros...

COAST GUARD IMMIGRATION RESTRICTOR. Those guys are always going to the beach at the wrong time of year...

"100 MISSION CRUSH" — for that first furlough home from FLYING SCHOOL

THE GOOD OLD ALL-PURPOSE M-1 BUCKET

The MARINE GALS... TEUFELHUND with chic...

The "DOCTOR LIVINGSTONE" makes every Dogface look like he built the PANAMA CANAL — well, maybe a foxhole

No doubt about who's got responsibilities in the WAVES and SPARS

ARMY NURSES allowed to wear new brown peaked cap on the street — and WACS get field cap for post duty — All goes well until dumb civilian mistakes one branch for the other....

The A.A.F. "DONALD DUCK"

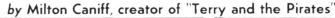

on DISH-FACED jokers this is MUR-DER!

What your mom wouldn't give for a matched set of six of these to meet the cooking vessel shortage

MILTON CANIFF

REMEMBER?

1/23/44

Male Call

by Milton Caniff, creator of "Terry and the Pirates"

I Dream Of Genii

I ALLA TIME SEE PITCHERS OF THIS HERE MISS LACE RUNNIN' CLOSE ORDER WITH SO-JERS... WHICH OUTFIT IS IT SHE BUDDIES-UP WITH, D'Y' RECKON?

WHY, ONLY TODAY I CABLED GENERAL MARSHALL, ASKIN' HIM TO CHECK ON THAT FOR ME...

...AW! Y'KIDDIN'...

SURE, SPORT!...THAT LACE BABE IS SORTA EVERY G.I.'S CHICK... YOU MIGHT RUN INTO HER ON A PASS INTO TOWN MOST ANYWHERE...DARWIN, BELFAST, ALGIERS, KUNMING, BOSTON, FORT WORTH, SEATTLE, KODIAK, INDIANAPOLIS — WHEREVER YOU HOPE TO HAVE A GOOD TIME...

I'D LIKE TO HAVE A GOOD TIME RIGHT HERE... BUT I SUPPOSE SHE'S NOT FOR GUYS WITH DIRTY EARS... AND NO HOPE OF A FURLOUGH...

I GUESS NOT... HMMM..... I MUST BE GOIN' NUTS! I'D SWEAR I SMELLED PERFUME JUST THEN...

MILTON CANIFF

1/30/44

Male Call

by Milton Caniff, creator of "Terry and the Pirates"

Rear Echelon Don Juan

2/6/44

Male Call by Milton Caniff, creator of "Terry and the Pirates" R. H. I. P. (Rank Hinders Impromptu Propositions)

2/13/44

Male Call

by Milton Caniff, creator of "Terry and the Pirates"

Support For Exposed Flank

Male Call

by Milton Caniff, creator of "Terry and the Pirates"

He'll Have To Go Through Chanel's

Male Call

by Milton Caniff, creator of "Terry and the Pirates"

What You Hear Is A Roomer

SERGEANT ANDERSON TO SEE MISSY!

OH, YES — PARDON ME, GENERALS....

SURELY, MISS LACE...

OH, SERGEANT, I'M SO GLAD YOU PHONED ME! THE HOTELS ARE SO CROWDED— YOU CAN SLEEP HERE WITH ME...

SERGEANT ANDERSON, I'D LIKE YOU TO KNOW--- SAY— WHAT'S THE MATTER WITH YOU JOKERS?

MILTON CANIFF

3/5/44

Male Call

by Milton Caniff, creator of "Terry and the Pirates"

Who Threw That Section Eight?

WHY DON'T WE CALL THE INFORMATION DESK AT THE STATION HOSPITAL, MISS LACE? THEY'LL KNOW...

GOOD IDEA!

WE'RE HAVING A BIG ARGUMENT OVER HERE THAT YOU CAN PROBABLY SETTLE FOR US.... HOW DO YOU SPELL 'CADUCEUS'?

U.S.A.M.D.

I DUNNO... WHAT OUTFIT IS HE IN?

MILTON CANIFF

3/12/44

Male Call

by Milton Caniff, creator of "Terry and the Pirates"

Nice Lines Of Communication

3/19/44

Male Call

by Milton Caniff, creator of "Terry and the Pirates"

Scents-ible Approach

HMMM — VELLY FANCY PLESENT, MISSY LACE! BIG COST!

YOU SAID IT... I'VE GOT AN IDEA...

HIYA, GENERAL? WHAT DO YOU HEAR FROM THE WIFE AND KIDS?

THEY'RE SWELL, MISS LACE!

THAT BOY WILL BE PLAYING A FAST TACKLE BEFORE LONG, GENERAL

I SHOULD KNOW BETTER THAN TO TRY TO BEAT THE BEST CHECKER PLAYER IN THE INFANTRY...

SORRY TO GET TO YOU LAST, GENERAL... BUT I ALWAYS ENJOY MY DESSERT MOST...

LATER

FUNNY THING, LIEUTENANT, I'VE NEVER KNOWN THE MEN IN THIS WARD TO SLEEP SO SOUNDLY...

3/26/44

Male Call
by Milton Caniff, creator of "Terry and the Pirates" **Must Have Come From Under The Rock Of Ages**

4/2/44

Male Call
by Milton Caniff, creator of "Terry and the Pirates" **Forecastle Armor**

4/9/44

Male Call

by Milton Caniff, creator of "Terry and the Pirates"

Son Of The Beach

4/16/44

Male Call

by Milton Caniff, creator of "Terry and the Pirates"

Not Afreud Of The Dark

4/23/44

Male Call

by Milton Caniff, Creator of "Terry and the Pirates"

Men Sometimes Go Nuts In The Army

Panel 1: I HAVEN'T BEEN AROUND, MISS LACE, 'CAUSE I GOT BUSTED AND CONFINED TO BARRACKS! I THOUGHT YOU MIGHT HELP ME MOURN... — WHY, SURE, GENERAL... PARDON ME — THERE'S THE DOOR BELL...

Panel 2: MISS LACE, I JUST GOT MY STRIPES — I THOUGHT YOU MIGHT LIKE TO HELP ME CELEBRATE! — WHY — AH — OF COURSE, GENERAL — BUT WE'LL HAVE TO MAKE IT A THREESOME — I HAVE A GUEST FROM THE 15th —

Panel 3: WELL, Y' DON'T WANTA FEEL TOO BAD, MAC... NO MORE RESPONSIBILITIES... YOU ONLY HAVE TO WORRY ABOUT YOUR OWN SELF — AND NOT EVERY GOLDBRICK IN THE OUTFIT... — LEMME GIVE Y' A TIP... MAC, THE FIRST TIME YOUR COMPANY COMMANDER CALLS YOU IN, GET THE CONVERSATION AROUND TO WHERE YOU SAY 'WAS THAT THE WAY YOU DID IT AT WEST POINT, SIR'?.. CHANCES ARE HE NEVER SAW TH' PLACE — BUT IT'LL TICKLE HIM SO HE'LL PUT Y' IN HIS GOOD BOOK!

MILTON CANIFF

Copyright 1944 by Milton Caniff, distributed by Camp Newspaper Service

4/30/44

Male Call

by Milton Caniff, creator of "Terry and the Pirates"

Very Low-gistics

Panel 1: JUST WHAT IS IT THE QUARTERMASTER CORPS DOES, GENERAL? — WHY, MISS LACE, DIDN'T YOU KNOW US QUARTERMASTERS REALLY LOOK AFTER ALL THE IMPORTANT STUFF IN THE ARMY?..

Copyright 1944 by Milton Caniff, distributed by Camp Newspaper Service

Panel 2: US GUYS ARE EXPERTS ON TRANSPORTATION, F'RINSTANCE!... WE REALLY KNOW HOW TO GET 'EM THERE...

Panel 3: AND WE GET 'EM FED! — US QUARTERMASTERS CAN ANTICIPATE EVERY EMERGENCY WHEN IT COMES TO SUPPLYING RATIONS — OH — AH... — JUST THE GOOD PROVIDERS, EH GENERAL..

Panel 4: YUH!... AH — MISS LACE D'YOU SUPPOSE YOU COULD PAY FOR THE MEAL AND THE TAXI... Y'SEE, I KINDA MISCOUNTED...

MILTON CANIFF

5/7/44

Male Call

by Milton Caniff, creator of "Terry and the Pirates"

G. I. Geneva

PEACE CONFERENCES
A.T.W.A.S. *

BUT, MR. JONES, I DON'T CARE IF YOU GO OUT WITH NO NECKTIE!

* AFTER THE WAR AND SIX ...

THIS JOB MEANS LONG HOURS AND ALL KINDS OF WEATHER—THINK YOU CAN TAKE IT?

TUNISIA, SICILY, ANZIO

I ONLY ASKED IF YOU'D LIKE A NICE BROWN SUIT

NO, NO...YOU SIT DOWN, HONEY! I'LL BRING YOUR DINNER TO THE TABLE!

AND THE SECOND THING I'M GONNA DO IS GET INTO A PAIR OF LOOSE PANTS

SAY — AREN'T YOU BLUE FLAME WILSON, THE FAMOUS FIGHTER PILOT?

I WAS AND I WANTA BUY A PORCH CHAIR — ONE THAT DOESN'T EVEN ROCK!

IT WAS ONLY THE 3:15 AIRLINER GOING OVER JUST AS THE FIRE SIREN SOUNDED

DADDY, WHY IS IT YOU NEVER TELL ME ABOUT TARAWA?

5/14/44

Male Call

by Milton Caniff, creator of "Terry and the Pirates"

Hooked By The Book

BUT, LOO-TENINT, I BIN FILLIN' MY CANTEENS.... I WAS ONLY GONE A FEW MINUTES...

YOU DID NOT ASK PERMISSION — THEREFORE YOU WERE ABSENT WITHOUT LEAVE! THE ARTICLES OF WAR SPECIFICALLY DESIGNATE THAT AS A COURT MARTIAL OFFENSE!

I MUSTA STEPPED IN A HOLE, LOO-TENINT! WHEN I COME UP MY RIFLE WAS GONE!

YOU LOST YOUR PIECE? LOSS OF GOVERNMENT PROPERTY IS SPECIFICALLY NOTED IN THE ARTICLES OF WAR AS A COURT MARTIAL OFFENSE!

BUT I KILT TH' NIP WOT WORE IT, LOO-TENINT! I KINDA THOUGHT MY KIDS WOULD LIKE T'HAVE--

ALL PUBLIC PROPERTY TAKEN FROM THE ENEMY IS THE PROPERTY OF THE UNITED STATES! THE ARTICLES OF WAR SPECIFICALLY STATE ...

I DON'T KNOW HOW MY GAL GOT IT THROUGH — BUT WE WON'T WORRY ABOUT THAT!... I'D OFFER THE LOO-TENINT A SWIG — BUT THE ARTICLES OF WAR SPECIFICALLY STATE THAT IT'S A COURT MARTIAL OFFENSE FOR AN OFFICER TO RECEIVE PRESENTS FROM THOSE UNDER HIS COMMAND!

5/21/44

Male Call

by Milton Caniff, creator of "Terry and the Pirates"

Knot Hole In Any Party Platform

5/28/44

Male Call

by Milton Caniff, creator of "Terry and the Pirates"

Tool-Happy Terminology

6/4/44

Male Call

by Milton Caniff, creator of "Terry and the Pirates"

It's Hard To Learn To Be A Glamour Boy

HOP IN, FELLAS! ALWAYS HAPPY TO PICK UP AN INFANTRYMAN...

LET THOSE INFANTRYMEN MOVE UP TO THE HEAD OF THE LINE...THE MEN FROM THE FOXHOLES DESERVE A BREAK...

THIS IS ON ME, GENTS! I GUESS A REDLEG SORTA OWES A DOGFACE A BEER NOW AN' THEN—JUST ON GENERAL PRINCIPLES...

ANY GUY WITH INFANTRY BLUE PIPING ON HIS CAP GETS FIRST CRACK AT A RIDE, AFTER THE AIR FORCES...GRAB A 'CHUTE AND CLIMB ABOARD!

YUH LATE, SEE! FOR W'ICH Y'CAN JIST FORM A LATRINE DETAIL AN' GIT T' DIGGIN'!.. Y' THINK I'M RUNNIN' A CLUCKIN' RECREATION CENTER?... BETWEEN REPLACEMENTS AN' FURLOUGHS THIS OUTFIT'S GETTIN' LIKE A CLUCKIN' P.O.E.! GET GOIN' LIKE I TOLD YUH!

....KINDA NICE TO BE HOME, AIN'T IT?

47 INFAN

6/11/44

Male Call

by Milton Caniff, creator of "Terry and the Pirates"

Charge Without Reconnaissance

WHAT'S THIS HERE? MISS LACE DANCIN' WITH A CLINKIN' CIVILIAN!

I ALWAYS THOUGHT SHE HAD SOME RICH 4F ON THE STRING... WHERE ELSE DOES SHE GET ALL THEM CLOTHES?

YEAH... AN' COME TO THINK OF IT, WHY AIN'T THAT JOADIE IN UNIFORM? HE LOOKS HEALTHY ENOUGH...

YOU SAID IT... THEY'RE COMIN' OFF THE FLOOR —WATCH ME NEEDLE HIM!

HIYA, BUB! HOW'S THINGS IN ESSENTIAL INDUS---

LACE! LACE! WHERE ARE YOU?

OH—THERE YOU ARE! I GOT SORTA PANICKY FOR A MINUTE!..DIDN'T SOMEONE SAY SOMETHING TO ME?

YES, GENERAL, IT'S A G.I. ALSO BACK FROM THE SOUTH PACIFIC... HE WANTS TO SHAKE YOUR HAND!

6/18/44

Male Call

Nice Legs On The T. O.

LOOKEE YONDER! REAL HARDWARE GENERALS.... IT'S THE WOLF PATROL WITH MERIT BADGES! COME IN AND WRINKLE YOUR PINKS, GENTLEMEN!

THIS IS NOT EXACTLY AN OFFICIAL VISIT, MISS LACE — BUT WE SORT OF REPRESENT OFFICERS GENERALLY....

DEAL 'EM AND WE'LL PLAY 'EM! WHAT COOKS WITH THE ACT OF CONGRESS SET?

FRANKLY, WE WOULD LIKE TO KNOW IF YOU DISLIKE OFFICERS? YOU SEEM TO DATE ONLY ENLISTED MEN...ARE WE POISON?

FAIR QUESTION!...NO, I'M NOT ALLERGIC TO BRASS...I COULD GO INTO A PITCH ABOUT THE O.D. JOKERS HAVING FEWER PRIVILEGES AND ALL THAT... BUT YOU KNOW THOSE REASONS

IT SOUNDS SORTA CORNY TO TELL IT, BUT I'VE GOT A JOB TO DO TILL YOU ALL GET BACK TO STRIPED NECKTIES!..YOU BRASSIES RATE A SALUTE FROM ALL E.M. — BUT JOE GEE OFTEN FORGETS THAT CIVILIANS WOULD LIKE TO TOUCH THEIR CAPS TO HIM, IF THEY KNEW HOW!... I'M HERE TO PROVIDE SOMEONE TO SALUTE HIM FIRST!...THEN HE PASSES IT ON TO YOU!... BUT DON'T BE DISCOURAGED —YOU MIGHT GET THE BREAKS ANYTIME...HMMM?

6/25/44

Male Call

It's A Kilt Tilt

IF Y'GOTTA HAVE A BREAKDOWN, THIS HERE STREET CORNER AIN'T A BAD PLACE!.. I'LL MATCH LEGS WITCHA FER PENNIES... I SAY THAT ONE'S A BLONDE

YOU WIN — I'LL CALL THE NEXT ONE...

REDHEAD!

NOPE — IT'S A BLONDE... Y'GOTTA CALL AGAIN — I'M TWO PENNIES UP ON YUH!

IT'S A WAC — A BRUNETTE!

RIGHT! NOW I'M ONLY ONE UP AND I CALL THE NEXT ONE...

ALL BETS ARE OFF!

7/2/44

Male Call

by Milton Caniff, creator of "Terry and the Pirates"

Practically A Signal Corpse

7/9/44

Male Call

by Milton Caniff, creator of "Terry and the Pirates"

Beachhead Feint

7/16/44

Male Call

by Milton Caniff, creator of "Terry and the Pirates"

Mess Consolidated

7/23/44

Male Call

by Milton Caniff, creator of "Terry and the Pirates"

Betwixt Wind And Water

7/30/44

Male Call

by Milton Caniff, creator of "Terry and the Pirates"

Perspective In Map Reading

8/6/44

Male Call

by Milton Caniff, creator of "Terry and the Pirates"

Everything Went Pink

8/13/44

Male Call

Contour Map (Note Magnetic Azimuths and Topographic Features)

8/20/44

Male Call

by Milton Caniff, creator of "Terry and the Pirates"

Mover-Slightly Beyond Prime

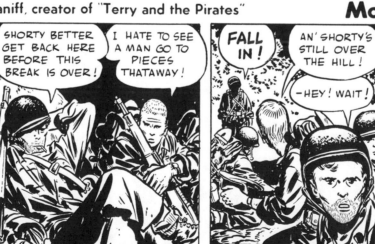 

8/27/44

Male Call

by Milton Caniff, creator of "Terry and the Pirates"

Anti-Personnel Bum

HOP IN!

THANKS, MA'AM, SAY, I THINK YOUR RIGHT FRONT TIRE IS SOFT...

NO — I GUESS IT'S OKAY!

WHEW! THAT'S A RELIEF! LATCH ON AND WE'LL ROLL...

FUNNY — THE OTHER GUYS AREN'T ASKING FOR RIDES TODAY... BY THIS TIME THEY'RE USUALLY PACKED IN HERE LIKE SPAM ON THE LAM...

MAYBE I'M SLIPPIN'!

9/3/44

Male Call

by Milton Caniff, creator of "Terry and the Pirates"

A.S.T.P. *(Apply Science to Propositioning)*

ANTHROPOLOGY REFRESHER CHART (FOR THE RETURNING SERVICE MAN WHO WISHES TO RESUME HIS EDUCATION AS SOON AS POSSIBLE...)

THIS IS A GIRL

"SPECIES AMERICANUS" (THE ALL-OVER OUTLINE IS THE SAME EVERYWHERE, BUT THE NORTH AMERICAN CLIMATE SEEMS TO PRODUCE DISTINCTIVE RESULTS)

SOME TYPES ARE READY SUBJECTS AND MAY BE PICKED UP AND FONDLED

NO RING — NO WRASSLE!

OTHERS ARE WARY UNTIL CERTAIN OF THE STUDENT'S ACTUAL INTENTIONS

THERE ARE AREAS IN WHICH THE STUDENT WILL FIND THE SPECIES IN ABUNDANCE... IN OTHERS THE FIELD MAY HAVE BEEN WORKED OVER BY LOCAL SCIENTISTS...

BEGINNERS ARE WARNED NOT TO BE MISLED BY THE GAUDY SURFACE COLORING OF SOME SUBJECTS... OFTEN THE MOST SATISFYING RESEARCH MAY BE CONDUCTED WITH PLAIN TYPES — ESPECIALLY THOSE WITH NESTS OF THEIR OWN...

MANY STUDENTS BECOME SO ATTACHED TO THE LITTLE CREATURES THEY DECIDE TO MAKE PERMANENT PETS OF THEM ... AT THIS POINT YOU THROW THE BOOK AWAY...

9/10/44

Male Call

by Milton Caniff, creator of "Terry and the Pirates"

Pets Beget Whet Threat

DO YOU MEAN THAT COMBAT TROOPS GO IN FOR SUCH CHILDISH DISPLAYS? TAKE THOSE THINGS DOWN!

SIR, THERE IS A CERTAIN PRACTICE AMONG THE MEN THAT I ---

OH, HELLO — YOU'RE THE REPLACEMENT THEY SENT ME, AREN'T YOU? — BEEN WAITING FOR A LULL TO HAVE A CHAT WITH YOU... I PROMOTED A COUPLE OF CIGARS — WILL YOU COME IN AND HAVE A SMOKE?

NOW, LIEUTENANT, WHAT WAS IT YOU WANTED TO SPEAK TO ME ABOUT?

9/17/44

Male Call

by Milton Caniff, creator of "Terry and the Pirates"

Dry Run — But All Under-water Shots

Y'SEE, MISS LACE — OUR GIRLS AT HOME HAVE SORTA GIVEN US A FAST BRUSH AN' WE THOUGHT IF WE COULD SEND 'EM SOME SNAPSHOTS OF US KISSIN' YOU THEY'D BE JEALOUS ENOUGH TO PUT US BACK IN THE NUMBER ONE SPOT! THEY LIVE IN DIFFERENT TOWNS — AND THEY WON'T KNOW WHO YOU ARE...

WE-E-LL... I GUESS IT'S A GOOD CAUSE ... OKAY, GENERALS!

NOW ME!

CLICK

AWRIGHT! SHIFT!

CLICK

WHAT IS THIS, A SERIAL?

MY TURN!

CLICK

ONE MORE, PLEASE!

WHEW! FIFTEEN OF THOSE POSES MAKES FOR A TOUGH WAR — HEY! THERE ARE EIGHT EXPOSURES ON THOSE ROLLS — AND THEY DIDN'T CHANGE FILM!

9/24/44

Male Call

by Milton Caniff, creator of "Terry and the Pirates"

Plain Identification

AWRIGHT! AWRIGHT! PUTCHA MONEY WHERE Y'MOUTH IS! I'VE SEEN THIS NEW DOUGHIE WORK!

Y'NUTS! SOME GOOD MEN HAVE TRIED IT...

THIS AIN'T NO ORDINARY CHICK, SON! I'LL RIDE WITH THE BABE!

NOBODY IN THIS OUTFIT'S BEEN ABLE TO MAKE IT SO FAR! I'LL TAKE FIVE AT THEM ODDS...

GIVE A LOOK! D'YOU THINK SHE'LL BE ABLE TO HOLD OUT ON A A-DO-NIS LIKE THAT THERE?

THEY SAY HE'S HAD OFFERS FROM HOLLYWOOD AFTER THE WAR!

THAT DON'T MATTER...I'VE TRIED IT — AND I AIN'T WORRIED ABOUT THAT MONTH'S PAY I GOT ON HER!

THERE HE GOES... Y'GOTTA ADMIT HE'S HIGH, HEP AN' HAN'SOME!

I'VE STILL GOT TEN OPEN THAT SAYS HE CAN'T SWING IT!

BUT, MISS LACE, MY REPUTATION'S AT STAKE! THERE'S BIG MONEY BET ON ME! COME ON, MISS LACE, GIVE A GUY A BREAK!

IT'S NO USE, GENERAL... I SIMPLY WILL NOT TELL YOU WHETHER 'LACE' IS MY _FIRST_ OR _LAST_ NAME!

10/1/44

Male Call

by Milton Caniff, creator of "Terry and the Pirates"

P/O Joe

WHAT GOT ME WAS THE WAY THEY KEPT COMIN'— WAVE AFTER WAVE...THEY WUZ AS GOOD AS ANY JAPANESE OL' HIROHITO HAS IN HIS IMPERIAL GUARD...

OH, DEAR... I'VE ALWAYS WANTED TO HEAR ONE OF THOSE PACIFIC VETERANS TELL OF HIS EXPERIENCES

I UNLIMBERED THE OL' SQUIRT BOX AN' THEY DIED LIKE FLIES ...BUT MORE CAME ON! I WAS GOIN' NUTS... I DUG AN' SQUIRTED AN SNIPED AT 'EM DAY AN' NIGHT... I WUZ EXHAUSTED...

THOSE AWFUL FLAME THROWERS! I SAW THEM IN THE NEWS-REELS! UGH!

FINALLY, IT WUZ THEM OR ME...I MADE ONE LAST TRY— THEN I SAID NUTS TO THIS— IF THEM BEETLES LIKE THE VEGETABLES IN MY VICTORY GARDEN _THAT_ WELL — I'LL GO TO THE A&P...

GOTTA RUN, JERRY — BRING THE MISSUS OVER...THE WIFE AN' KIDS WUZ ASKIN' FOR 'EM ONLY TODAY! IF I CAN GET A RENEWAL ON MY B-BOOK WE'LL HAVE A PICNIC SOMEWHERES...

10/8/44

Male Call

by Milton Caniff, creator of "Terry and the Pirates"

What A Standing Operating Procedure

10/15/44

Male Call

by Milton Caniff, creator of "Terry and the Pirates"

Jump Mistress

10/22/44

Male Call

The Flavor Lasted and Lasted

I REMEMBER A MOVIE I SAW WHEN I WAS A KID...THIS YANK SO-JER HAD SOME GUM—AN' HE TEACHES THIS FRENCH GIRL HOW TO CHEW IT! HE DID ALL RIGHT!...

WELL, THAT MIGHT GET US A LOOK AT MADAME LAMI'S TWO DAUGHTERS! —EVERYBODY IN THE OUTFIT'S HEARD OF 'EM—BUT NOBODY'S SEEN 'EM!

BONE SWAR, MADAME! ...JE HAVEZ HERE BEAUCOUP CHEWIN' WAX... MEBBE SO VOTRE JUNE FILLIES WOULD LIKE SOME OF SAME? TASTEZ TRAY BONE!

CHEWING GOM? MAIS NON, M'SIEU!

PORE QUAH, MADAME? GEE WHIZ ...

THAT'S HOW I GOT THE DAUGHTAIRS, SOLDAT!

10/29/44

Male Call

How Vargan One Go With These Things?

I'M A BUSY MAN! WHY DON'T YOU TAKE SOME OF THIS PETTY DETAIL OFF MY HANDS?

YES, SIR!

MORE PETTY DETAILS... TAKE CARE OF THEM YOURSELF!

THE CAPTAIN HAS ORDERED ME TO HANDLE PETTY MATTERS

THAT'S MORE LIKE IT!

HOW LONG HAVE YOU WORKED FOR MR. PETTY?

11/5/44

73

Male Call

by Milton Caniff, creator of "Terry and the Pirates"

Truth and Consequences

11/12/44

Male Call

by Milton Caniff, creator of "Terry and the Pirates"

Miscue At Staging Area

11/19/44

Male Call

by Milton Caniff, creator of "Terry and the Pirates"

Cooked By A Hash Mark

THIS IS A REAL PLEASURE, ZINKY — OR SHOULD I SAY CORPORAL ZINKERMANN? WE READ ABOUT THE MEDAL IN THE PAPERS, BUT WE WANT TO HEAR THE STORY FIRST HAND FROM OUR OWN EX-FELLOW WORKER — DON'T WE FOLKS?

OH, YES!

GO ON, ZINKY!

WELL, IT WASN'T SO MUCH...

WE WERE ROLLIN' UP FAST ON THE SOISSONS ROAD...

THE SOISSONS ROAD! — BOY! I'LL NEVER FORGET THE NIGHT WE MOVED UP ON SOISSONS IN '18... WE WENT INTO THOSE WOODS WITH NO SLEEP AND NO CHOW...

...JERRY WAS CAUGHT NAPPIN' — BUT WE HAD TO SLUG FOR EVERY YARD WE TOOK... IN THE WHEAT FIELDS WE RAN INTO THE BOCHE WIRE...

½ HOUR LATER

...BY THE TIME THEY RELIEVED US I WAS WALKIN' IN MY SLEEP... SAY! WE'LL HAVE TO BE GETTIN' BACK ON THE JOB!... GLAD YOU DROPPED IN, ZINKY... COME IN ANYTIME — WE'RE MIGHTY PROUD OF OUR HERO!

MILTON CANIFF

Copyright 1944 by Milton Caniff, distributed by Camp Newspaper Service

11/26/44

Male Call

by Milton Caniff, creator of "Terry and the Pirates"

Leg Log

THE NAVY'S SHIP AND AIRCRAFT NOMENCLATURE IS OFTEN CONFUSING TO LANDSMEN... SINCE SAILORS THINK OF THEIR SHIPS AS FEMALES, THIS CHART WILL MAKE IT SIMPLER TO UNDERSTAND SOME OF THOSE GROUPS OF LETTERS...

Copyright 1944 by Milton Caniff, distributed by Camp Newspaper Service

AR (ALWAYS RELIABLE) SHE'S THE MOTHERLY SORT — NOT GLAMOROUS, BUT NICE TO TURN TO WHEN YOU NEED SYMPATHY

PT (PARTY TYPE) SHE LIKES TO GO PLACES AND DO THINGS... SHE STAYS UP TILL THE SUN GOES DOWN!

GOOD CONDUCT!

AO (ALL OUT) SHE'LL GET DIRTY WITH YOU IF YOU DON'T FEND HER OFF

DD (DANCING DEVIL) A FAST OPERATOR... SHE'LL ROLL YOU IF YOU DON'T LOOK LIVELY

SS (SILENT SENDER) WHEN YOU GO OUT WITH HER SHE HOLDS YOU SO CLOSE YOU SELDOM EVEN COME UP FOR AIR!

MILTON CANIFF

BB (BROAD BEAM) SHE'S BIG AND TOUGH — AND A GOOD GAL TO BE WITH IN BANDIT COUNTRY...

CV (CHARMING VIXEN) SHE LIKES TO TOSS OFF A FEW NOW AND THEN... NO MATTER HOW OFTEN YOU RUN OUT ON HER, SHE'S ALWAYS WILLING TO TAKE YOU BACK...

FOR LUBBERS ONLY

DD - DESTROYER
PT - PATROL TORPEDO BOAT
SS - SUBMARINE
BB - BATTLESHIP
AO - OILER
CV - AIRCRAFT CARRIER
AR - REPAIR SHIP

12/3/44

Male Call

by Milton Caniff, creator of "Terry and the Pirates"

Kipling Didn't Know American Soldiers

ON Y'WAY, SOLDAT! I'M HERE TO PRESENT MISS LACE WITH A NAZI FLAG I BROUGHT HER —AND NO HOT WEATHER DOGFACE IS GONNA RED LINE ME!

FALL BACK AND GROUP UP WITH YER MAM-ZELS, MUD-EATER! THERE WASN'T NO DAMES ON MY ATOLL A-TALL AND I AIMS T'PRESENT THIS JAP OFFICER'S SWORD TO THE DREAM SCHEME THAT KEPT ME OUTA SECTION EIGHT!

WHY— WITH ONE HAND I COULD—-- SAY, IS THAT A SURE ENOUGH, GEN-YOU-WINE JAP SWORD?

SURE IT IS! —BUT BEFORE I HANG Y' TEETH ON Y' VOITIBRAY, LEMME HAVE A QUICK DOUBLE O AT THAT NAZZY FLAG...

GEEZST—THE KID BROTHER WOULD GO NUTS OVER THIS HERE SUMMER-RYE SWORD!

HMM—THE OLD MAN WOULD GET A BOOT OUTA A CAPTURED HEINIE FLAG

SAY, MAC, HOWZ ABOUT A BEER WHILEST WE TALK THIS OVER ?..

I WUZ JUST ABOUT T'SUGGEST THAT VERY SAME THING!

OH, WELL, A GIRL HAS TO PLAY THE PERCENTAGES!

MILTON CANIFF

12/10/44

Male Call

by Milton Caniff, creator of "Terry and the Pirates"

Tetched-nition Fifth Grade

WELL, GENERAL, YOU GOT ROTATED AND HERE YOU ARE WITH RIBBONS AND EVERYTHING!... I'LL BET YOU HAVE PLENTY TO REMEMBER ...

OH, DAT I HAVE, MISS LACE, DAT I HAVE...

BUT ONE T'ING KEEPS BODDERIN' ME... ONE DAY DIS HERE O-REE-EN-TASHUN AWFISSER WAS LECTURIN' AT US ABOUT A BATTLE NAMED WATERLOO... VER-EE INTERESTIN...

...JUS' DEN COMES A AIR RAID A-LERT —WE HIGH-TAILED IT FOR THE DITCHES...

AN' I NEVER DID FIND OUT WHO WON DAT DERE BATTLE!

MILTON CANIFF

12/17/44

Male Call
by Milton Caniff, creator of "Terry and the Pirates"   **Daddy, Would They Bust A Marine For This?**

MISS LACE, THEY TELL ME YOU HAVEN'T BEEN SEEN AROUND WITH MANY MARINES — SO I THOUGHT I'D COME ALONGSIDE AND GIVE YOU A BREAK...

WELL, THAT'S MIGHTY WHITE OF YOU, GENERAL! — FIND YOURSELF A BATTLE STATION WHILE I RIG TO REPEL BOARDERS!

SHALL WE GET DOWN TO LASHIN' LIPS RIGHT AWAY — OR WOULD YOU WANT ME TO GIVE YOU A FILL-IN ON MY FLUFF LOG?...LESSEE, THERE WAS THAT TRIM BIM IN DAGO...

LOOK, GYRENE, WHEN YOU BUILD UP THIS KIND OF PRESSURE SOMETHING'S GOT TO GIVE — AND IT'S NOT GOING TO BE ME...

YOU MEAN YOU'RE TURNIN' DOWN A MARINE?

IT'S A MAGGIE, BRAGGY... YOU SEVENED OUT... NO DEAL!

DON'T TAKE IT SO HARD, PARD... I WON'T TELL A SOUL...

12/24/44

Male Call
by Milton Caniff, creator of "Terry and the Pirates"   **Air-Ground Co-operation**

GEE, GENERAL, I'M SORRY TO HEAR YOU CAME OUT WITH COMBAT FATIGUE... IS IT BAD?

IT'S TOUGH, MISS LACE... ANY SUDDEN SOUND MAKES YOU JUMP!

BANG! BANG!

OH, GOLLY!... CAN I GET YOU ANYTHING?

DON'T MOVE... JUST LET ME STAY LIKE THIS... IT GOES AWAY AFTER AN HOUR OR SO!

12/31/44

Male Call

by Milton Caniff, creator of "Terry and the Pirates"

Well, Slip My Cable

1/7/45

Male Call

by Milton Caniff, creator of "Terry and the Pirates"

Cold Dressing

1/14/45

Male Call

by Milton Caniff, creator of "Terry and the Pirates"

As He Was

1/21/45

Male Call

by Milton Caniff, creator of "Terry and the Pirates"

Is He Trapped Or Is She A Mouse?

1/28/45

Male Call
by Milton Caniff, creator of "Terry and the Pirates"

Message Center For The Main Body

2/4/45

Male Call
by Milton Caniff, creator of "Terry and the Pirates"

Snap-in by Harley-Davidson

2/11/45

WOULDJA LOOK AT OL' CHOCKLE —STILL IN THERE PITCHIN'!

HE DIDN'T EVEN MOVE WHEN THE LOOTENINT YELLED TO HIM THAT WE COULD FALL BACK!

I'LL NEVER CHEW OLD CHOCKLE OUT AGAIN AFTER THAT PERFORMANCE! MOVE UP WITH THE ARMOR—

CHOCKLE ISN'T STIRRING...MAYBE HE'S HIT! HAINES, SEE IF YOU CAN GIVE HIM A HAND!

THE LOOTENINT THINKS YOU'RE A HERO FOR STICKIN', CHOCKLE! YOU'LL RATE A COMBAT BADGE FOR THIS... IT MUSTA TOOK GUTS!

PLEASE DON'T TELL NOBODY— BUT I PUT MY LEGGIN'S ON BACK-WARDS AGIN...! I COULDN'T WALK 'CAUSE I'M HOOKED ONTO MYSELF!

2/18/45

THAT ROTATION IS FER ME! GEEZST, I KIN HARDLY WAIT!

SERGEANT, CALL IN THAT MAN WHO'S YAPPING ABOUT ROTATION ...

YEZZR

LOOK, SOLDIER, I KNOW THIS PLACE IS NO PARADISE OF THE PACIFIC, BUT YOU'D BETTER FORGET THAT ROTATION STUFF — BECAUSE IT MAY BE A LONG TIME BEFORE YOU CAN BE SENT HOME ...

BUT, SIR, Y'GOT ME WRONG! IF YOU WOULD SO KINDLY STEP OUT HERE A MINUTE...

THAT'S WHAT I WUZ TALKIN' ABOUT...

POST THEATRE TONIGHT at 1830

COPIA (The HIP) EFICAZ MAMA en CAMA

2/25/45

Male Call
by Milton Caniff, creator of "Terry and the Pirates" **Grilled Chicken on Three-Decker, Well Browned**

3/4/45

Male Call
by Milton Caniff, creator of "Terry and the Pirates" **Briefs for Observation Mission**

3/11/45

Male Call

by Milton Caniff, creator of "Terry and the Pirates"

Personnel Officer, Female, Civilian, Hep

3/18/45

Male Call

by Milton Caniff, creator of "Terry and the Pirates"

She Looks Different Without Bangs

3/25/45

Male Call

by Milton Caniff, creator of "Terry and the Pirates"

Once Over Slightly

BEA-VER! SOME OF THE HAY GROWN IN THIS WAR WOULD MAKE ANY BARBER ITCH !....

DOES HE PUT IT INSIDE OR OUTSIDE THE SACK?

INSIDE—SO HE DON'T SUCK IN AN' STRANGLE WHEN HE SNORES

MARINE SNIPER COVER DELUXE

OXYGEN MASK SPECIAL... DANGEROUS IF CAUGHT IN A SLIDING COCKPIT CANOPY!

THE SGT. MAULDIN MAT

TRIM THAT BEARD OR SHAVE IT OFF!

?

THE ONLY GOOD DEED HITLER EVER DID WAS TO PUT THE SMELL ON THE WORLD WAR I O.C.S. TOOTHBRUSH!

YANKEE INGENUITY

DARLING!

LET'S SEE YOUR A.G.O.! THE MAN I MARRIED HAD FIVE O'CLOCK SHADOW, BUT NOT A BLACKOUT!

Copyright 1945 by Milton Caniff, distributed by Camp Newspaper Service

MILTON CANIFF

4/1/45

Male Call

by Milton Caniff, creator of "Terry and the Pirates"

Snappy Story

MISS LACE, THE TROUBLE IS, YOU LEAD A FELLER ON — THEN, JUST WHEN HE THINKS YOU'RE WILLING, YOU BACK OUT!

I SUPPOSE YOU'RE RIGHT, GENERAL...

LET'S USE THE SOFA... I'LL SLIP INTO SOMETHING MORE COMFORTABLE AND BE RIGHT WITH YOU

OH BOY OH BOY!

I KNEW YOU'D LOOK AT 'EM IF I ASKED YOU NICE... THIS HERE IS ONE I TOOK OF THE KID SISTER ON MY LAST FURLOUGH...

MILTON CANIFF

4/8/45

84

Male Call

by Milton Caniff, creator of "Terry and the Pirates"

Just Keep The Suit, Bub

DON'T LOOK SO NERVOUS, MEN! DO YOU WANT TO LIVE FOREVER?

OKAY, TAKE A BREAK!

THIS JUST CAME FOR YOU...

HE'S FAINTED

WHAT WAS IN THE LETTER?

IT'S FROM HIS DRAFT BOARD! "GREETINGS..."

4/15/45

Male Call

by Milton Caniff, creator of "Terry and the Pirates"

Physi-oh-thera-beaut-ics

WHAT'S THE PITCH, GENERAL... ARE THINGS BREAKIN' A LITTLE ROUGH TODAY?

YOU DON'T NEED A BLUEPRINT, LADY... WHEN MY GIRL GETS A LOOK AT THE SINGLE WING FORMATION SHE'S NOT GONNA YELP WITH JOY!

IS SHE ABOUT MY HEIGHT AND BUILD? HERE, GIVE IT A FAST GO-ROUND, JUST FOR SIZE...

?

HMM—YOU TAKE UP THE SLACK WELL AND YOU HAVE A STEADY SQUEEZE...JUST HOLD YOUR BREATH! NOW, LET'S FIRE A ROUND FOR EFFECT!

WHAT HAPPENED? YOU WERE SCRAPIN' BOTTOM THIS MORNING!

I JUST QUALIFIED WITH THE MM-M-M-ONE!

4/22/45

Male Call

by Milton Caniff, creator of "Terry and the Pirates"

Permanent Party with Temporary Advantage

AND THAT'S THE WAY IT IS, MISS LACE...I DID SO WELL IN MY CLASS THEY MADE ME AN INSTRUCTOR—I HAVEN'T BUDGED OFF THIS POST!

IT MUST BE SATISFYING TO KNOW YOU'VE TURNED OUT GOOD MEN!

OH, SURE, BUT HERE I AM—WHILE MANY OF MY EX-PUPILS HAVE COMPLETED THEIR TOURS...SOME OF THEM WERE SUCH RAW KIDS I HAD TO HELP THEM WRITE LETTERS TO THEIR GIRLS...

WELL, WHADYA KNOW...

IF IT AIN'T THE OL' PERFESSOR!...WITH A STACK O' PINK LIKE I DREAMED ABOUT ALL OVER THE ISLANDS! UNLATCH, GATCH, AN' LEAVE ME TUNE HER IN ON MY MEMOIRS...

FALL BACK AND REGROUP, GENERAL! I'D LOVE TO HEAR YOU READ OFF YOUR RIBBONS, BUT TONIGHT I'M APPLE-POLISHING WITH TEACHER! HE CAN'T TELL ME ABOUT HIS OPERATIONS, BUT THERE'S PLENTY OF GO IN THE MAN WHO GAVE YOU THE KNOW—FROM THIS ANGLE I CAN'T TELL WHETHER THAT COLD SPOT IS A UNIT CITATION OR JUST PLAIN BRASS BUTTON!

4/29/45

Male Call

by Milton Caniff, creator of "Terry and the Pirates"

You Never Know Where the Front Is

NOW THAT THE OLD OUTFIT IS BUSTED UP, I HATE TO LEAVE THE SARGE...HE WAS TOUGH, BUT HE KNEW HIS BUSINESS...

YEAH—REMEMBER THAT RAID WHEN HE GRABBED THEM TWO KRAUT MACHINE GUNNERS WITH HIS BARE HANDS?...

FUNNY ABOUT THE SARGE—HE WAS ALWAYS BELLERIN'—BUT EVER SINCE WE GOT ON THE BOAT HE'S BEEN SORTA QUIET...

YEAH—ALL THROUGH PROCESSIN' HE HARDLY SAID A WORD...

HE'S GETTIN' OFF HERE—FUNNY, HE NEVER DID SAY WHERE HE LIVED...GOLLY, HE AIN'T EVEN SAYIN' GOOD-BYE TO NOBODY...

THAT AIN'T LIKE HIM...HE MUST HAVE SOMETHIN' ON HIS MIND... WELL, THERE GOES A FIGHTIN' MAN!

SO—YOU'RE BACK! I SUPPOSE YOU ACTUALLY ENJOYED YOURSELF ON THAT CAMPING TRIP, WHILE ME AN' THE KIDS WAS STRUGGLIN' TO GET ALONG!...YOU KNOW, DON'T YOU, THAT OTHER MEN YOUR AGE GOT DISCHARGES? THEY BEEN BACK HERE MAKIN' GOOD MONEY WHILE YOU WAS TRYIN' TO BE A HERO! AN' SPEAKIN' OF MONEY: WHERE'S THAT ALLOTMENT BEEN? I HAVEN'T HAD A CHECK SINCE WE MOVED! YOU'D THINK THE GOVERMINT WOULD KEEP TRACK OF THINGS LIKE THAT...

5/6/45

Male Call

by Milton Caniff, creator of "Terry and the Pirates"

And He Used To Welcome Cover

WE BROUGHT YOU FROM THE CANTEEN TO THIS FASHION SHOW TO OBTAIN A SOLDIER'S REACTION ON CURRENT MODES! A STENOGRAPHER WILL TAKE DOWN YOUR REMARKS...

Copyright 1945 by Milton Caniff, distributed by Camp Newspaper Service

HE KEEPS REPEATING..."AND IN ITALY I USED TO COMPLAIN THAT IT WAS JUST ONE MOUNTAIN AND ONE VALLEY AFTER ANOTHER"

5/13/45

Male Call

by Milton Caniff, creator of "Terry and the Pirates"

Bitter Glitter

I WANT THIS UNIFORM PRESSED — AND THERE IS NEW GOLD LACE, OR BRAID, AS YOU PROBABLY CALL IT, IN THIS ENVELOPE — WILL YOU SEW IT ON AND GET IT BACK IN AN HOUR? I HAVE A SPEECH TO MAKE DOWN IN THE BANQUET ROOM! LIVELY NOW!

HOKAY! — SPECIAL FOR YOU, BOSS...

55 MINUTES LATER...

COME IN! COME IN!

KNOCK KNOCK

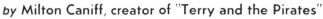

HOT STUFF, EH, BOSS?

Copyright 1945 by Milton Caniff, distributed by Camp Newspaper Service

5/20/45

(Note to Editors: Because of many requests for biographical material on Milton Caniff, this story is sent to you this week in place of "Male Call" which will be resumed next week.)

Milt Caniff Draws Lovely Ladies for a Living

This reverie in black and white features Milton Caniff, creator of "Terry and the Pirates" and "Male Call" a father to some of the most languorous ladies in comic strip history. Grouped around the artist are some his creations (you may recognize them) and the gremlins which forever haunt his drawing boa

Milton Caniff (pronounced like a sneeze) is a brown-haired 38-year-old Irishman who works 7 days a week, 365 days a year drawing beautiful women.

These women are incorporated in 2 of the most successful comic strips of our time, "Terry and the Pirates" and "Male Call." "Terry" appears daily in 175 civilian newspapers and the European and Italian editions of Stars and Stripes. "Male Call" is issued weekly to more than 2500 official service newspapers on the Camp Newspaper Service mailing list.

The 2 strips are produced in a glassed-in studio high in the Catskills in Rockland County, N. Y., where Caniff may be found working every night. There, too, may be found Burma and Lace and April Kane and the Dragon Lady and the other comely wenches Milton's quill and brush have produced . . . as well as the artist's real life helpers, his wife, his dog, his 2 assistants.

He Talks With Either Hand

He is an unusual artist in many respects. First, he works hard and loves it. Second, he does his own drawings, plots his own stories, writes his own dialogue. Third, he's ambidextrous. He plays golf, writes and eats soup with his right hand. He draws, paints and plays billiards with his left.

Caniff started drawing beautiful women about the time the other kids in his home town of Hillsboro, Ohio, were drawing mustaches on streetcar posters. He pursued this passion through high school and 4 years at Ohio State University and later on the Columbus Dispatch where he worked until 1930. In 1932 he began an adventure strip, "Dickie Dare," and in 1934 "Terry" was born.

"Terry" was a hit from the be-

Caniff and Col Phil Cochran (He's Flip Corkin in "Terry") survey one of Milt's strips at the artist's studio in Rockland County, N. Y.

ginning. First, it was a spine-tingling adventure strip, full of hair-raising action and crisp dialogue. And, secondly, it was full of beautiful dames. This combination put "Terry" over faster than a pitchman selling lemonade at MalayBalay.

Burma Was a Lady

First of the Caniff cuties to catch the public eye was Burma, a blonde and slangy number with hips like a boa constrictor and a purple past. Burma has sashayed her way through the "Terry" strip off and on for the last 10 years, growing progressively more desirable.

Another sensational Caniff lovely is the Dragon Lady, a slo-eyed Eurasian, with a phenomenal figure and a background as shady as a back alley in the Casbah.

Then there is the lady known as Lace, the GIs little playmate and heroine of Caniff's "Male Call" strip. Lace, a home bred beauty with overtones of Lana Turner and Marlene Dietrich and undertones of Jean Harlow and Lauren Bacall, is the sweetest little dish on the TO to thousands of servicemen from Calcutta to Canarsie.

The Man Loves Work

In addition to producing "Terry" and "Male Call," Caniff, who was rejected for service because of a bum leg, has made a couple of major contributions to the war effort. He illustrated OCD manuals for M Day on how to put out incendiary bombs before Pearl Harbor. When war came he did a full page on what to do in the event of an air raid. Later, he illustrated the Soldier's Pocket Guide to China and at least one of his "Terry" strips—the one in which Col Flip Corkin briefs Terry on the duties of an AAF officer, has found its way into posterity through publication in the Congressional Record. Profits from his "Male Call" book, recently published, will go to Army Emergency Relief.

All this keeps Caniff as busy as a man with St Vitus dance in an ant hill, but the man loves work. It doesn't bother him a bit.

"In fact," says he, "I have only one problem. I write all my own stuff. Then I have to go back and draw it, and I write myself into some of the damndest difficulties."

6/3/45

Male Call

by Milton Caniff, creator of "Terry and the Pirates"

Bum Check at a Blood Bank

5/27/45

Male Call

by Milton Caniff, creator of "Terry and the Pirates"

Protective Coloration

6/10/45

Male Call

Side Issue

I'M AFRAID MISS LACE IS GETTING SORT OF WAR WEARY

YEAH... SHE'S BEEN ON HER TAIL TOO MANY TIMES...

ONE OF HER TIPS IS KIND OF NICKED

SHE HASN'T BEEN RIGHT SINCE THE CAPTAIN SCRAPED HER BELLY THAT NIGHT

HEY!

...I KNOW MISS LACE AND I WON'T LET YOU FELLERS TALK ABOUT HER THAT WAY! SHE'S A NICE GIRL — SHE'S--

WHAT'S EATIN' THIS JOKER?

Miss LACE

6/17/45

Male Call

Critical Point

GOSH, FELLERS, CAN YOU IMAGINE THEM PALM TREES?

Bahnhof KREU

AND ALL THEM HOOTCHIE HULA GALS RUNNIN' AROUND...

AN' LAYIN' OUT ON THEM WHITE BEACHES — AN'--

Y'OUGHTEN TO DO IT, JAKE – AFTER ALL, HE WENT THROUGH THE WHOLE THING WITH US!

6/24/45

Male Call

by Milton Caniff, creator of "Terry and the Pirates"

Target of Opportunity

7/1/45

Male Call

by Milton Caniff, creator of "Terry and the Pirates"

Natural Cover

7/8/45

Male Call

by Milton Caniff, creator of "Terry and the Pirates"

All Together They Spell "Musher"

7/15/45

Male Call

by Milton Caniff, creator of "Terry and the Pirates"

Global Strategy"—So Round; So Firm . . ."

7/22/45

Miss Lace and Caniff Make Television Debut

By Camp Newspaper Service

CNS-Yank photo—Friedman

After Milton Caniff drew Lace, NBC produced Conover model Dorothy Partington, who portrayed the GI heroine in a television broadcast. Model Partington admitted she doesn't look much like Lace.

Miss Lace, who has hit as many Army camps as most GIs, turned up in a new spot the other night and made her television debut over NBC's New York station, WNBT. Chances are the event went unnoted by Lace's many followers, because there are but 6,000 receivers in the station's 50-mile radius.

The occasion was an interview of Milton Caniff, Lace's creator, by Julian Bryan, a travel lecturer. Caniff drew our gal's portrait as he answered questions, and the whole thing was televised.

As he pencilled in Lace's sleek hair, Caniff explained that in the early days of Army publications, there was a need for a humorous feature, which he offered to fill.

Giving her eyes, he said the feature had to have a gag in each insertion, rather than follow a continuity, "because soldiers move around quite a bit." Caniff then drew Lace's lips, and told of his fan mail.

"Sometimes chaplains object to her," he said, "but I tell them the boys need Lace. Sometimes the chaplains go overseas for a while and write me that I am right."

After Caniff finished his drawing without a model, which he seldom uses, NBC produced one in the person of a Dorothy Partington.

An NBC press agent had Dorothy pose for pictures in alluring, Lacey attitudes. Afterwards, the press agent asked her:

"Did anyone ever tell you you look like Lace?"

In surprise, she replied: "Oh my no."

EDITORS: This feature is a substitute for the regular CNS 'Male Call' strip. 'Male Call' will be resumed next week. **7/29/45**

Male Call

by Milton Caniff, creator of "Terry and the Pirates"

Dreamboat Barnacle

YOU SAY YOUR DREAMS MAKE YOU ILL?

YES, SIR, YOU KNOW HOW IT IS... YOU'RE SNOOZIN' AWAY AND THIS BEE-YOU-TEE-FUL DOLLIE SHOWS UP IN FULL COLOR...

NO SHADOW BOXIN' PRELIMINARIES —SHE'S FULLY PACKED AN' WEARIN' SOMETHIN' SOFT AN' COOL WHICH YOU CAN'T SEE THROUGH, BUT WHICH YOU CAN TELL BY THE WAY SHE RIPPLES HER ELBOWS — YOU KNOW WHAT I MEAN, SIR?

MM-H-M GO ON...

WELL, SHE SLIDES INTO CLOSE ORDER WITH YOU —THEN YOU'RE FEELIN' LIKE 85 POINTS...AND, OH, BOY, SIR...YOU FOLLOW ME, DON'T YOU, SIR?

SURE — BUT WHY SHOULD A DREAM LIKE THAT MAKE YOU ILL?

THAT'S THE KIND THE OTHER GUYS ALWAYS TALK ABOUT! I KEEP DREAMIN' I JUST FLUNKED THE FIFTH GRADE AGAIN — AN' I'M SICK OF IT!

8/5/45

Male Call

by Milton Caniff, creator of "Terry and the Pirates"

Can't Ship See Rations

YOU E.T.O. MEN WHO HAVE BEEN RE-ASSIGNED TO THE PACIFIC ARE VETERANS —AND YOU WANT NO CHICKEN FROM ME ON HOW TO FIGHT A WAR... HOWEVER,

ASSEMBLY AREA COMMUNICATIONS ZONE

...EACH THEATRE HAS IT'S PECULIAR PROBLEMS... I DID A TOUR OUT THERE AND THE BOSS FIGURES I MIGHT GIVE YOU THE WORD ON SOME OF THE CHANGES THAT WILL TAKE PLACE IN YOUR S.O.P.

THAT IS CHANGE NUMBER ONE!

8/12/45

Male Call
by Milton Caniff, creator of "Terry and the Pirates"
Ay, There's The Rub!

MISS LACE, I WON'T TELL YOU NO LIE... I'VE BEEN AWAY FROM WIMMIN FOR SO LONG I AIM TO LOG ME SOME LIP TIME— RIGHT UNDER YOUR NOSE!

SOMEBODY'S GIVEN YOU A BUM STEER, GENERAL—I WON'T BE STAMPEDED!

COULD YOU BE PLAYING THE PERCENTAGES?

Copyright 1945 by Milton Caniff, distributed by Camp Newspaper Service

8/26/45

Male Call
by Milton Caniff, creator of "Terry and the Pirates"
"You Are Going To A Strange Country"

YESSIR, YOU'DA THOUGHT THE CG WROTE MOST OF THE AR HIMSELF! HE HAD US ALL PO'D HALF THE TIME... WELL, THIS DAY HE STUCK US OUT AHEAD OF OUR OP AND THE MOS WENT BLOOIE! WE HAD EVERY GEE ON A BAR OR M 1...THE ENTIRE T/O FROM THE CO TO THE LOWEST PFC GOT A PH, THANKS TO THAT ONE 88!

OH, DEAR, MISS LACE, IT'S WONDERFUL TO HAVE EARL HOME FOR AWHILE ...BUT I DON'T UNDERSTAND HALF OF WHAT HE SAYS ...

IT'S THOSE ARMY ABREVIATIONS! ...I HAVE AN IDEA ...

Copyright 1945 by Milton Caniff, distributed by Camp Newspaper Service

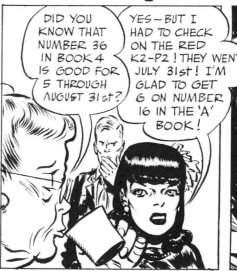

DID YOU KNOW THAT NUMBER 36 IN BOOK 4 IS GOOD FOR 5 THROUGH AUGUST 31st?

YES—BUT I HAD TO CHECK ON THE RED K2-P2! THEY WENT JULY 31st! I'M GLAD TO GET G ON NUMBER 16 IN THE 'A' BOOK!

POCKET GUIDE TO the UNITED STATES

9/2/45

Male Call

by Milton Caniff, creator of "Terry and the Pirates"

Permanent Party Game

9/9/45

Male Call

by Milton Caniff, creator of "Terry and the Pirates"

No Chicken, Inspector

9/16/45

Male Call

by Milton Caniff, creator of "Terry and the Pirates"

Combat Point

WELL, NOW THAT THE WAR'S OVER I HOPE THE HOTELS AND RESTAURANTS WILL SOON BE CLEARED OF THOSE DREARY PEOPLE IN UNIFORMS — WITH ALL THOSE SILLY RIBBONS!

...REALLY, I DON'T SEE WHY SOLDIERS AREN'T KEPT IN THEIR CAMPS WHEN THEY'RE NOT FIGHTING, RATHER THAN BEING ALLOWED TO OVERRUN ALL THE DECENT PLACES... AND THEIR <u>WOMEN</u>! — WELL, MY DEAR ...

FOR THE TAXES WE PAY, ONE WOULD THINK THE GOVERNMENT COULD PROVIDE A PLACE FOR THOSE UNHAPPY LOOKING FEMALES AND THEIR CHILDREN ONE SEES IN THE PUBLIC PARKS... OF COURSE THE CREATURES WEAR RINGS, BUT---

SHALL I WAIT HERE FOR THE WAGON, MANAGER?

WHAT WAGON?

9/23/45

Male Call

by Milton Caniff, creator of "Terry and the Pirates"

Whew CQ

GEE, I'LL BET YOU'RE GLAD TO HAVE HIM BACK, MISSUS SMITH

YOU CAN SAY THAT AGAIN...

LOOKIT HIM IN THERE SLEEPIN' SO PEACEFUL...

HMM...

I REALLY STOPPED TO ASK IF YOU'RE GOIN' DOWN TO MARKET...

NO — NOT TODAY — HE'S LIABLE TO WAKE UP AND WANT SOMETHING...

9/30/45

Male Call

by Milton Caniff, creator of "Terry and the Pirates"

Braille Detail

10/21/45

Male Call

by Milton Caniff, creator of "Terry and the Pirates"

Selective Service Entrance, Bub

10/28/45

Male Call

by Milton Caniff, creator of "Terry and the Pirates"

Well, You Save Money That Way

11/4/45

Male Call

by Milton Caniff, creator of "Terry and the Pirates"

There's A Kid with Crust

11/11/45

11/18/45

11/25/45

12/2/45

12/9/45

Male Call

by Milton Caniff, creator of "Terry and the Pirates"

Class B, Class A's

12/23/45

Male Call

by Milton Caniff, creator of "Terry and the Pirates"

Home Front Hodgepodge

1/6/46

Male Call Dividend
by Milton Caniff

Reprinted by Request

Male Call

by Milton Caniff, creator of "Terry and the Pirates"

How To Tabulate A Rate

MISS LACE, LET'S PLAY A GAME! THE MR. JOHNSON WE'RE HAVING DINNER WITH IS FROM MY OUTFIT AND JUST OUT OF UNIFORM... SEE IF YOU CAN TELL WHETHER HE WAS A BRASSIE OR A GEE-EYE!...

I'LL TRY— BUT THOSE PIN STRIPES CAN BE DECEPTIVE!

Copyright 1945 by Milton Caniff, distributed by Camp Newspaper Service

AFTER DINNER...

YOUR FRIEND WAS A HARDWARE BOY!

YOU HAD A 50-50 CHANCE OF GUESSING RIGHT... WHAT CAUSES YOU TO THINK HE WAS AN OFFICER?

OH, THERE WERE THE USUAL THINGS!.. YOU KEPT JOCKEYING TO GET ON HIS LEFT AS WE WALKED... YOU GOT INTO THE CAR FIRST... HE DROPPED MY ARM PREPARING TO RETURN A SALUTE EVERY TIME WE PASSED ENLISTED PERSONNEL...

WHEN WE HIT THAT PLUSH JOINT, HE PEEKED FIRST AT THE PRICE SIDE OF THE MENU!.. ANY GEE WHO VENTURED IN THERE WOULD KNOW HE HAD MORE THAN ENOUGH CASH OR HE'D HAVE STAYED AWAY... BUT MOST OF ALL I NOTICED HOW HARD AND OFTEN YOU SLAPPED HIM ON THE BACK AND CALLED HIM "PAL"— AND HOW HE'D OPEN HIS MOUTH—THEN SHUT IT AND SIT RESIGNED... ELEMENTARY, MY DEAR GENERAL!

MILTON CANIFF

1/13/46

Male Call

by Milton Caniff, creator of "Terry and the Pirates"

Redeployment

HONEY, REMEMBER HOW YOU USED TO WRITE ABOUT LIVING IN ICE WATER UP TO YOUR WAIST—AND HOW YOU COULD TAKE IT?

YEAH, BABY, I USED TO SURPRISE MYSELF...

Copyright 1946 by Milton Caniff, distributed by Camp Newspaper Service

I RECALL ONE LETTER IN WHICH YOU TOLD ABOUT A DEMOLITION JOB! ...ALL THE TNT IN THE WORLD UNDER YOU—READY TO BLOW—BUT SOMEHOW YOU WEREN'T SCARED

UH-HUH — I NEVER FIGGERED THAT ONE OUT... I WALKED RIGHT INTO THAT ROPED OFF AREA AS IF IT WAS A MARBLE GAME...

HONEY— DO YOU THINK COMING HOME HAS CHANGED YOU MUCH?

I DUNNO, BABE... WHY?

I HOPE IT HASN'T— BECAUSE I LEFT THE OUTSIDE CELLAR DOOR OPEN... THE WATER PIPES FROZE AND BROKE, THE WATER FLOODED THE BASEMENT AND PUT OUT THE FIRE IN THE GAS FURNACE! I DROPPED THE FLASHLIGHT IN THE WATER TRYING TO TURN OFF THE GAS... AND I HOPE YOU WERE TELLING THE TRUTH IN THOSE LETTERS...

MILTON CANIFF

1/20/46

by Milton Caniff, creator of "Terry and the Pirates"

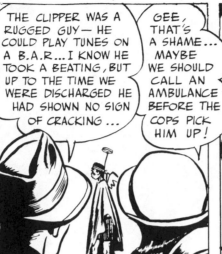

1/27/46

by Milton Caniff, creator of "Terry and the Pirates"

2/3/46

Male Call

by Milton Caniff, creator of "Terry and the Pirates"

Cross Word Puddle

ALL RIGHT, YOU EXTRAS, GET DOWN AND WALLOW IN THAT MUD...

REMEMBER, THIS IS A WAR PICTURE! REALISM! THAT'S WHAT WE WANT— STARK, RAW REALISM!!

MAC, THAT SLOP WOULD PLAY HOB WITH THE RHEUMATIZ I GOT IN THEM HOLES IN THE EYE-TALIAN MOUNTAINS... I RECKON I'LL DO WHAT I WANTED TO DO THEN — TURN IN MY SUIT...

WHAT'S THE MATTER, EXTRA? ...MAKIN' SO MUCH MONEY YOU'RE SCARED OF A LITTLE MUD?

I KNEW THERE WAS SOMETHING ELSE I ALWAYS WANTED TO DO AT THE SAME TIME I TURNED IN MY SUIT!

2/10/46

Male Call

By Milton Caniff, creator of "Terry and the Pirates"

For Whose Good?

D.H. LOGAN
Dept. Mgr.

I DON'T UNDERSTAND THESE VETERANS, ELLA! ...YOU'D THINK A YOUNG MAN WHO HAD BEEN A MERE CORPORAL ON A PACIFIC ISLAND FOR MONTHS AND MONTHS WOULD BE HAPPY IN A POSITION AS MANAGER OF AN ENTIRE DEPARTMENT, BUT TODAY THAT LOGAN CHAP CAME TO ME AND SAID HE WANTED TO BE TRANSFERRED TO THE FOUNDRY—FOR THE GOOD OF THE FIRM!

2/17/46

2/24/46

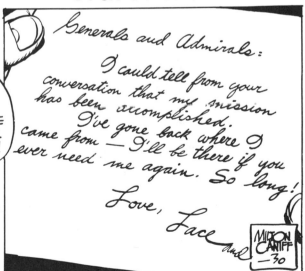

3/3/46

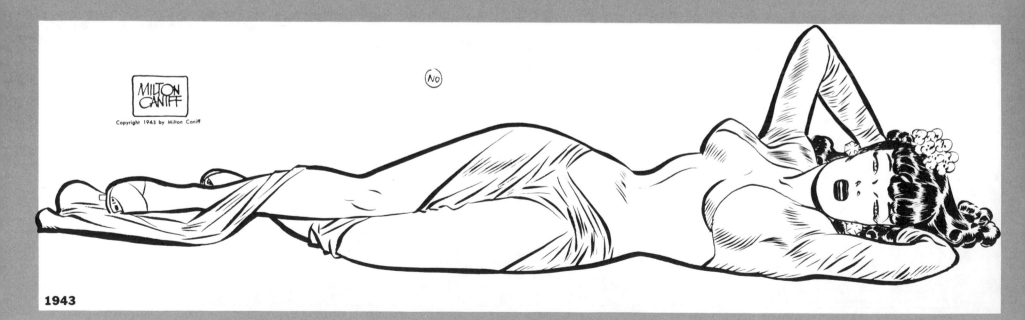

OH, BOY! NO REVEILLE! NO POLICE UP! NO CLOSE ORDER DRILL!

MILTON CANIFF

WHAT'S CHUCKLIN' YOU, LACE?

THEY SHOULD HAVE MORE DISTINCTIVE INSIGNIA ON THOSE WAC UNIFORMS!

1944

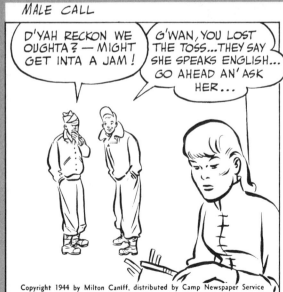

D'YAH RECKON WE OUGHTA? — MIGHT GET INTA A JAM!

G'WAN, YOU LOST THE TOSS...THEY SAY SHE SPEAKS ENGLISH... GO AHEAD AN' ASK HER...

AH — MY BUDDY AN' ME — AH — THERE'S SOMETHIN' WE ALWAYS WANTED TO FIND OUT...

IS IT TRUE THAT CHINESE WOMEN...

MILTON CANIFF

...USED TO BIND THEIR FEET ?

1944

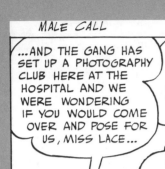

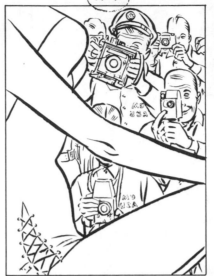

I NEVER SEE SUCH A HAND FOR WORK AS THAT SMITH BOY! DON'T YOU RECKON WE COULD SET OUR DISCHARGED HEE-RO TO DOIN' SOMETHIN' A MITE EASIER?

YORE RIGHT, PAW —I'LL PUT HIM T' SORTIN' APPLES...

JEST PUT TH' BIG ONES IN THESE BASKETS —THE MIDDLE SIZE ONES IN THEM BASKETS —AN' TH' LEETLE ONES HERE...THROW THE ONES WITH ROTTEN SPOTS IN THE BIN... I'LL BE BACK T' SEE HOW YORE AGITTIN' ON ...

LATER

COME QUICK! TH' SMITH BOY IS AWRITHIN' AN' AHOLDIN' HIS HEAD!

WHAT AILS Y', SON? Y' GOT A SPELL O' THAT THERE BATTLE FAT-TEEG?

NO —IT'S MAKIN' THEM **DECISIONS** THAT'S WHUPPED ME!

Copyright 1945 by Milton Caniff, distributed by Camp Newspaper Service

1945

WHAT'S THE MATTER, EARL, YOU NERVOUS ABOUT BEIN' THE LOCAL HERO? YOU'RE SMOKIN' LIKE A HUTMENT STOVE...

I'M MORE NERVOUS ABOUT THE OWNER OF THE MILL SENDIN' HIS LIMOUSINE TO MEET US AT TH' TRAIN! I'VE NEVER SAT IN A HEAP LIKE THIS BEFORE ...

LATER...

THE YOUNG MILITARY GENTLEMAN LOOKED SO FINE RIDING THE CAR, SIR

GLAD TO DO IT! GLAD TO DO IT! ALWAYS GLAD TO BE OF SERVICE TO THE TOWN...

YES, SIR, GIVES ME A GLOW... I THINK I'LL TELL PUTNAM TO DRIVE SLOWLY ON THE WAY TO THE MILL...THE GOOD PEOPLE WOULD PROBABLY LIKE TO HAVE A LOOK AT ME...

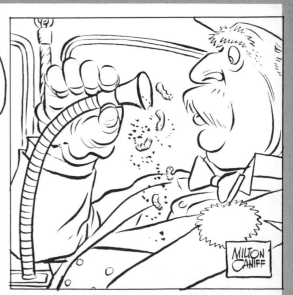

Copyright 1945 by Milton Caniff, distributed by Camp Newspaper Service

1945

IN THIS DRAWING FOR 'EDITOR AND PUBLISHER,' CANIFF BADE FAREWELL TO HIS WARTIME ENDEAVORS AND COMMENTS ON THE HOUSING SHORTAGE IN THE U.S. (1946).

MILTON CANIFF ENDED "MALE CALL" IN 1946, BUT THAT WAS NOT THE END OF MISS LACE. SHE CONTINUED TO APPEAR ALMOST ANNUALLY FOR THE NEXT 35 YEARS IN SPECIAL DRAWINGS FOR MILITARY REUNIONS AND VARIOUS PUBLICATIONS. THE PORTRAIT ABOVE IS FROM THE COVER OF "AIR FORCE" MAGAZINE, 1957. THE DRAWING AT RIGHT IS FROM A 1962 AIR FORCE ASSOCIATION PROGRAM COVER, AND THE DRAWING AT FAR RIGHT IS A DRAWING THAT APPEARED ON THE FRONT PAGE OF "SAM," AN ARMED FORCES NEWSPAPER, IN 1978.

119